Jon Tobelman

2.95

GREAT CHURCHES OF TODAY

GREAT CHURCHES OF TODAY

Outstanding Congregations
Their Leaders
Their Program
Their People

by the staff of DECISION

World Wide Publications
Minneapolis, Minnesota

Photos of U.S. and Canadian churches by Åke Lundberg.
Australian church photos by Donald A. Gee.

For information address World Wide Publications, 1313 Hennepin Avenue, Minneapolis, Minnesota 55403.

Library of Congress Catalog Card Number: 73-84956.

Introduction

"The Christian church," says Myron Augsburger, "is not a static institution, but men and women who flesh out in daily life the meaning of faith and the reality of the risen Christ." To read about a local congregation that is fulfilling this concept is an exciting experience. In these pages the editors of DECISION have brought together a series of profiles of viable, soul-winning churches that are making an impact on their communities. Most of the churches are large in membership. The principles on which they are built are Biblical and sound; that is why they have grown. Our purpose however has been not to commend but to describe.

Originally published as a series of articles in DECISION, these chapters have been edited for publication in book form and in some instances details have been brought up to date. Treatment has been popular rather than scholarly, yet we believe the book will make a substantial contribution to present day ecclesiology simply by tracing the planting and growth of flourishing congregations. In each church, as the reader will soon discover, the spiritual emphasis has been primary.

An effort has been made to achieve geographical and denominational representation, but the primary emphasis has been placed on the stature of the local church itself. To the pastors and staffs of the various churches goes our appreciation for help in obtaining the information that created the stories. Most of them were drafted originally by William Carey Moore during his tenure as assistant editor of DECISION. The Australian chapter was written by Helen Caterer. Mr. George M. Wilson, business manager of the Billy Graham Association, and Mr. Lee Riddle and Mr. DeWayne Herbrandson, were responsible for initiating the volume and seeing it through the press. They were assisted by Mrs. Randa Noble.

THE EDITORS

Contents

The Peoples Church

1

THE PEOPLES CHURCH
CHARTERED

1

The Peoples Church

Toronto, Canada

Toronto: a sprawling metropolitan giant, ocean port, financial capital of all Canada boasting the third largest stock exchange in the world. To The Peoples Church, Toronto affords an unending abundance of its chief stock in trade — people: 2,200,000 of them. Each year 400 to 500 of these Canadians exchange their sins for the righteousness of the Savior Jesus Christ, and receive their first shares in God's Kingdom, at the great interdenominational church established in 1928 by Oswald J. Smith.

Toronto's five boroughs form a tapered rectangle spreading 26 miles along Lake Ontario, and north from the lake 2½ to 5½ miles. To the early Huron Indians this was "the land of plenty," "a meeting place," long before the colonial governor, John Graves Simcoe of Upper Canada, established a settlement in 1793. Today it is the eastern terminus of the interprovincial pipeline and a host to major industries in wide divergence — printing, aircraft, meat packing, farm implement manufacturing. Its university is Canada's largest. How prudent of God to choose the site of this vigorous metropolis to build a church with the world upon its heart!

On the Sunday of my visit in Toronto, Dr. Smith, snowy-haired founder of The Peoples Church, drew me aside. He looked like a saint ready to meet his Lord — clear-eyed, erect in morning coat, kindness beaming from his face. "We thank God," he said, "for the gift he has given us in 'Dr. Paul.' I can truly say I'm seeing things we never dreamed of."

But what struck the visitor to The Peoples Church in the 1970s were the things that *were* dreamed of — including a grand total of 404 missionaries serving in the field under a $400,000 world mission budget. "The missionary work without doubt has made The Peoples Church great," Dr. Smith reflected. "For many years, each time our people gave one dollar for the home work, they gave seven for foreign work." Since 1928 the church has raised $7,000,000 for missions.

A member of the young Evangelical Fellowship of Canada, The Peoples Church is an independent congregation, and the missionaries it supports serve under 41 agencies in 66 countries around the world. During 1969 the congregation contributed $634,481 toward the church's program. Of this amount, 66.7 per cent went to missions.

Dr. Paul Brainerd Smith, younger son of Oswald and Daisy Smith, became the pastor of The Peoples Church in January, 1959, after engaging in evangelism on five continents and serving for seven years as an assistant to his father. Dr. Paul, who never remembers a time when he was not headed for the ministry, did not want to become associated with The Peoples Church. "I had watched the course of many successful men whose sons attempted to follow in their footsteps," he recalled, "and I was very much aware that the work would probably decline after Father left it."

He attributes the healthy growth that the church is now experiencing in part to the way in which his father resigned. "So far as the local work is concerned," Oswald told his son, "it is over to you!"

When Dr. Paul became pastor the congregation was beginning to take on the appearance of a middle-aged and older people's church. "We hadn't yet lost the crowds, but the Board of Managers decided to move where the people were."

The choice of a new location proved to be a wise one. Situated on a prominent avenue in rapidly growing North York Borough, the church today is a half-mile off East-West Throughway 401 and just minutes from the Don Valley Parkway that whisks Torontonians in and out of the business district 13 miles distant.

The present structure was erected in 1962 with about half of the funds realized from the sale of the old Bloor Street property. Sunday School development became a primary goal in the new location. By 1969 the Sunday School had increased to an average attendance of 1,400 pupils, the largest in Canada. The following year the auditorium was enlarged to seat 2,500 people.

The program of The Peoples Church involves 3,500 persons from week to week. Not until the sixties did the church invite people to "join," and today only about 1,200 are members. "We think of the church as a workshop rather than a showcase of saints," says Dr. Paul. The church's minister of education is the Reverend Robert Watt, D.D., of Edinburgh, Scotland, who has assisted the Drs. Smith for 15 years. The Reverend Elmer S. McVety is minister of visitation and evangelism.

Gospel singing would have to be a great tradition in any church whose founding pastor composed 1,200 hymns and Gospel songs, including "The Song of the Soul Set Free," "Then Jesus Came," "The Glory of His Presence." The man who is building on this foundation is a product of The Peoples Church, David E. Williams. Trained at Bob Jones University, the Royal Conservatory in Toronto and the University of Toronto, Williams was called to The Peoples Church as minister of music from a Southern Baptist church in Arkansas in 1960.

Today Williams directs the church choir, a 16-voice chorale, the Teen Tempos and a 40-piece orchestra which accompanies congregational singing Sunday nights. He writes and arranges much of the music and heads a faculty of ten accomplished musicians who conduct The Peoples Church School of Music. On occasion the choirs combine with Dr. Paul for a "song sermon" that packs the auditorium on Sunday night.

What holds the 150 college-age young people who participate in the church's ministries? "Three things," replies Dr. Paul. "First, we try to talk sense, and we find it can be done within a Biblical concept. Second, we keep the program interesting and (to choose a word I often use) exciting. And third, they hold each other." Dr. Paul himself is a graduate of McMaster University. After studying in the United States he later took his seminary training at Emmanuel College, a United Church of Canada-related institution in Toronto.

How does Dr. Paul, who is not "in business to preach to empty pews," make churchgoing exciting? Edward Dartnell, a food caterer who drives 25 miles to church from Etobicoke, and who says "the church changed the lives of my two boys," tells about the time the pastor once tried to lure a horse onto the platform. In a more conventional role, for nine Sunday nights in 1969 Dr. Paul invited a representative of a religious cult to speak for a half-hour before the service. One of the speakers was a prominent

A church with a world-wide passion, Peoples Church is probably supporting more missionaries than any other single congregation. Spearheading the church's life are the founding pastor, Dr. Oswald J. Smith (seated at right) and his son, Dr. Paul B. Smith, below.

"God is dead" theologian. Each Sunday night following such a visit, Dr. Paul answered from Scripture the cultist teaching of the week before.

One night he let a jukebox blare from the platform "to illustrate the type of music to which teen-agers are listening"; then he preached. He also uses song and cartoon sermons.

Dr. Paul gives his people a consistent pulpit diet of strong Biblical teaching, yet accepts the criticism that The Peoples Church is a "three-ring circus." "Remember," he warns, "the gimmick is simply the window dressing that brings them into the store, and what we do after they get here is to expose them to the Word of God."

Nowhere is the circus aspect more in evidence than in the youth work. And that is as it should be. "Ringmaster" is H. Verd Matts, an insurance man who has become a confidant of youth. His mind spins off programs under the pressure of the keen-minded company he seeks to stay ahead of. "To know young people you must know the home," says Matts. "When you've lost personal contact you're through." After devoting his life to young people for 25 years, he believes the church must provide "a place where young people can grow spiritually, where they can bring their unsaved friends, train for church leadership and enjoy fellowship." Activity involves Living Teens (ages 12-14), Teens for Christ (15-17) and Challengers (18-25) each week of the year, following a general monthly schedule of sports, outreach to youth, Scripture study and discussion, and service to the church.

"We're not producing programs because we're a big church," Matts points out. "We're producing programs because we're interested in youth. He gestured toward the chair opposite him in his tiny office. "Dennis Walsh sat there and rededicated his life to Christ. He and Gary Sanson have since worked out a constitution and bylaws for a car club. The members challenge each other's driving record on a point system, work on cars, and are building a 'rod' for racing. Each Christian boy in the club takes the personal witnessing course."

This church with the world as its parish draws all classes. One of its elders, who organized a "Men for God" group, is T. G. McCormack, president of Dominion Stores, Canada's largest supermarket chain. Arne Ylitalo, another elder, is a mechanic of Falcon Truck Lines. A Finn with an Italian wife, he remembers Easter Sunday, 1966, for that evening as he was leaving The

Peoples Church Dr. Watt met him and led him to Christ. Dr. Watt also prayed with their two children when they confessed faith in Christ.

In 1967 Dr. Paul trimmed the world mission conference to two weeks and brought in 150 missionaries from the societies that receive support from the church. "We have found," says Dr. Paul, "that missionary work is a lot more realistic when our people rub shoulders with the missionary. It has had a direct effect on the giving and it has enabled us to pray much more intelligently for our overseas work."

Founder's Week, held each fall, may take the form of a Bible conference, a prophetic conference or an evangelistic crusade. In 1969 it was a youth crusade that reached almost five hundred teen-agers each night; 90 of them made decisions for Christ. A children's crusade ran concurrently. The church hired 12 buses to pick up children at 36 schools and bring them to church. "We had almost fifteen hundred kids each night," says Dr. Watt. "There were over two hundred decisions for Christ from that group, but on top of that we believe we reached a great many homes. Parents would call us and say, 'This is something we've always wanted for our children and we haven't been able to find it.'"

Dr. Paul rates the church's literature ministry of equal importance with Founder's Week and the world mission conference. "We try to make Christian books available to the people and when we have services on week nights we seldom fail to promote some book," he says. Dr. Oswald Smith edits *The Peoples Magazine* and oversees the distribution of his 35 books (now condensed to 14 permanent volumes). Dr. Paul has written ten books.

Dr. Oswald Smith's books have been translated into 70 languages. "We get the most amazing reports of conversions and blessing through the books," Dr. Smith said, "and to that I am giving the last years of my life." In 1970, while he filled a demanding schedule of 20 mission conferences in the United States and an evangelistic crusade in Sweden, he continued to extend a book ministry behind the Iron Curtain. "The books are now in almost every country of Eastern Europe. We have just finished getting them into Bulgaria and Poland. The 280 Protestant churches still open in Poland distribute these books throughout the breadth of the land."

So there it is: a great church built on the priority of missions, on music, on youth, on evangelism, on literature, on hard work; but above all, on the faithful preaching of the Bible as the Word of God.

The irony is that The Peoples Church might never have "happened" had not Oswald Smith been turned down as a foreign missionary. After his conversion in the Torrey-Alexander Toronto campaign of 1906, he offered himself as a candidate to a mission board and his qualifications were rejected. "The only thing for me to do," he decided, "is to send out others."

Which he did.

Coral Ridge Presbyterian Church

2

Coral Ridge Presbyterian Church

Fort Lauderdale, Florida

Sunny ocean beaches, miles of scenic waterways, thousands of yachts, swaying palms and clean, clean air . . . stucco bungalows and lots of churches . . . expanding industrial parks and the *Queen Elizabeth I* . . . seat of the fastest-growing county in the eastern United States: this is Fort Lauderdale.

One city statistic, however, will never be listed in the official Chamber of Commerce brochure. It concerns Fort Lauderdale's incoming tide of followers of the Lord Jesus Christ, caused largely by what is happening at the Coral Ridge Presbyterian Church, the most rapidly expanding Presbyterian congregation in America. The Reverend D. James Kennedy, D.D., is pastor of this church which has grown from 17 to 2,005 members.

Coral Ridge's facilities do not breathe "greatness" unless one is anticipating the $6-million structure to be erected on Federal Highway 1 in north Fort Lauderdale. Coral Ridge is perhaps the only church ever to operate between two fire stations, one of which has been converted into a Teen Tower and Christian elementary day school.

The size of the church's 1970 budget — $756,000 — was no index to its spirituality. But the ability of the congregation to give that much, spurred directly by one stewardship sermon a year, does hint that Coral Ridge has something. Thirty per cent of the nondesignated budget went to missions and benevolences.

The Christian education program of the church has won national recognition, but the staff is gearing itself for an even more promising future ministry. Squeezed into classroom space it outgrew long ago, the Sunday School averages 800 pupils in attendance by holding some classes at 9:30 a.m. and others at 11:00. Miss Glenda Delmar, director of Christian education, organized a Midweek School of the Bible in the fall of 1970 to supplement the adult Sunday School program.

The Wednesday night school is part of a family night program which ministers to 400 children and adults weekly. Following prayer meetings, parents devote an hour to doctrinal and Biblical studies led by Dr. Kennedy, two of the staff ministers — Archie Parrish and Ed Johnson — and Jim Wilson, an accountant with "tunnel vision" for Christian education. The church opened 200 small Bible studies in homes during the 1970s to follow up those Floridians, mostly adults, who are receiving Christ through the ministry of the church's 300 evangelists.

In 1969 a newspaper editor in Missouri wrote to the church, describing how he had been won to Christ by a team of visitors from the church while he was in Florida. He pledged a substantial amount a month to support the church's witnessing program and enclosed a paid-up contract for a year's radio time on a local station for Dr. Kennedy's sermons. "I want to hear that Gospel on the air every week," he wrote.

Twenty-four hundred people, in three morning services, *do* hear it each Sunday. Watching the church-goers lined up outside the edifice, one man who recently moved to Florida from Texas remarked, "It's like they're giving something away." He was closer to the truth than he imagined. White-coated ushers quietly and efficiently guide worshipers to their seats. A few black faces can be seen in the congregation. (Membership at Coral Ridge is open to persons of all races.)

The church puts much thought and much ardor into its Sunday services. The 75-voice choir calls a capacity crowd of 800 people to worship with a rousing anthem of praise. An air of expectancy and excitement is evident as the assembly confesses its faith through creed and hymn. Superb engineering carries the sound of Dr. Kennedy's voice — even his whisper — to every pew. The pastor's dramatic involvement with the Scripture text makes a high moment of worship out of the reading. His messages are conversational, persuasive, free of clichés; evening sermons are verse-by-verse Biblical expositions.

Robert O. Brooks, production manager for a local radio station, directs the choir and writes the choral introits and responses. He acknowledges that "the singing at Coral Ridge has brought people back to church when the preaching did not." His choristers seem to be as much at home with Beethoven and Bach as they are with "How Great Thou Art."

Mrs. Diane Spargo, soprano soloist, touched the pulse of her church's true greatness: "Evangelism is what Coral Ridge is all about," she stated. In February of 1970, 170 pastors came to Fort Lauderdale from 30 states and Canada for the church's fourth annual evangelism clinic (850 others were turned away). In March Tyndale House (Wheaton, Illinois) published Dr. Kennedy's textbook *Evangelism Explosion.* Gospel Films, Inc., of Muskegon, Michigan, released a full-color movie on the church's evangelistic thrust.

The church is sharing the wealth of its evangelistic know-how through clinics and "daughter" clinics. Dr. Kennedy tells of one Michigan pastor who has held two clinics for 85 fellow pastors. The Associate Reformed Presbyterian Church has adopted the Coral Ridge plan for the denominational evangelistic program.*

The son of a Chicago salesman, James Kennedy was managing an Arthur Murray dance studio in Tampa when God shattered his self-sufficiency with one question: *"Suppose that you were to die tonight and stand before God and he were to say to you, 'Why should I let you into my heaven?' what would you say?"* The voice belonged to the late Dr. Donald Grey Barnhouse, radio preacher on "The Bible Study Hour."

On that Sunday morning, standing in his pajamas by his bedroom radio, James Kennedy decided to stop trusting in his own ability to live a successful life, and to trust Jesus Christ. A few months later he sensed God was calling him into the ministry; he enrolled at the University of Tampa to complete preparation for seminary. Before leaving for Columbia Theological Seminary in Decatur, Georgia, his wife, Anne, who had grown up in the church, saw her need of a personal relationship with Christ, and took her stand beside her husband as a new Christian. In 1959, when the Everglades Presbytery invited them to form a new church in Fort Lauderdale, they were ready.

Prospects, however, were dubious. The presbytery had selected a site that had become known as "Larson's Folly." It consisted of weeds, sand and coconut palms. Forty-five people gathered in a school cafeteria to hear Kennedy's first sermon on June 21, 1959.

**Coral Ridge Church is affiliated with The Presbyterian Church in the United States ('Southern')*

CORAL RIDGE
PRESBYTERIAN
CHURCH

ral Ridge Church has set a brilliant example in lay evangelism that
s been copied by hundreds of churches around the world. Pastor James
nnedy is seen seated at lower right during the singing of the choral
them at a morning service.

"I preached evangelistically," reflected the pastor, "and though I had taken all of the courses offered at seminary on evangelism and read many books besides, I found that the sophisticated people of Fort Lauderdale did not respond to my message. After eight or ten months the congregation had dwindled from 45 to 17. I was a most discouraged young minister."

About that time he was invited to preach in evangelistic services in Decatur. "Happy to get away from my Fort Lauderdale fiasco, I accepted the invitation," he says. But when the pastor informed Dr. Kennedy that they would be going out morning, noon and night to present Christ to people in their homes, he was "petrified." The next morning, "after my stumbling attempts," Kennedy recalls, "the pastor took over the conversation and in about 20 minutes brought the man to Christ." For ten days he watched the pastor lead some fifty persons to Christ. "I went back to Fort Lauderdale a new man, and began to do just what I had seen done. People responded. Soon dozens, scores, and then hundreds accepted Christ."

Kennedy realized that there was a limit to the number of people he could visit himself, so he began to train others. He organized a class, taught them six lessons and sent them out. "They all went home terrified!" Kennedy says. He expanded the instruction period to 15 weeks, but so far as he knows, not one of the laymen brought anybody to Christ through the classroom approach. "One day it struck me like a bolt of lightning," he says. "I had sat in classes for three years but had not learned how to witness until someone trained me 'on the job.' So I began a program which has continued for the past eight years, taking out one individual until he has confidence to witness to others, and then another, and another. After the people are trained, they in turn can train others."

The number of evangelists at Coral Ridge has reached 300, but the goal is 1,000. Dr. Kennedy has not dispensed with the classroom, but he majors in on-the-job training. Two programs, each four and a half months long, are conducted annually. Trainees for the visitation program are selected from the church membership. At a kickoff banquet Dr. Kennedy secures commitments to train for home evangelism. Then each Wednesday morning or Thursday night, trainees and trainers meet at the church and fan out by threes to visit.

"We have found that sending two trainees with each evangelist expedites the work," says Kennedy. "Also, to send two women into a modern metropolis at night is exceedingly risky. That is why we go out by threes."

Once they arrive at the home (usually the visit is paid to persons who have attended services at Coral Ridge), the trainer directs the conversation in a friendly manner from secular interests to the church and to spiritual realities. On each visit the evangelist attempts to do three things: (1) find out where the person is spiritually; (2) present the Gospel; and (3) bring that person to a commitment to Christ. The trainees learn to assume responsibility for presenting the Gospel. To reduce dropouts and encourage each other, the teams complete every visitation outing with a report session back at the church.

"Talk about the abundant life!" exclaims Clark Bennett, a salesman and a trained evangelist. "When one of these Christians is used to win another to Christ, it's like a rocket blasting off from Cape Kennedy."

I met the second man Dr. Kennedy had trained on a personal basis, Dr. Freeman Springer, a dentist who has led someone to Christ nearly every week for seven and a half years. Dr. Springer still recalls the night he received Christ after a very short visit by the Kennedys. "For the first time in years I slept like a baby," he says. "It seemed as if the cares of the whole world had dropped from my shoulders. I woke up the next morning and remarked to my wife, 'This is wonderful! You and I will be together for eternity.'"

The Reverend Archie Parrish directs the follow-up program of the congregation, a sizable task in a church whose evangelists brought approximately nine hundred persons to profession of saving faith in Christ in 1969. The program actually begins in the home when the decision is made. The spiritual "parent" gives the new believer a simple Bible study and arranges to meet him in church the following Sunday. The new Christian is invited to the next church membership seminar, which Dr. Kennedy holds each quarter, and is introduced to a sponsor. "We ask the sponsor to pray daily for the new convert," says Mr. Parrish, "to become acquainted with him and his family, to sit with him in church and introduce him to others." With such "little lassoes of friendship," Coral Ridge infuses fresh blood into the mainstream of its membership. The result is mutual growth and continuing renewal.

No measure of the greatness of the Coral Ridge Presbyterian

Church can be taken without recognizing the sons and daughters whom this church has "prayed" into God's work. In 1969 during a week of prayer the Reverend "Sim" Fulcher, youth pastor, suggested that the church ask God to lead ten of its members into full-time service that year. Two days before the year ended, the tenth man called Dr. Kennedy to announce he was presenting himself as a candidate for the ministry. In January of 1970 during the week of prayer 400 Coral Ridge members arrived at church at 5 a.m. each day to spend two hours praying and establishing goals for 1970. Already the church has given birth to two mission churches, both pastored by men who accepted Christ and received their call to the ministry at Coral Ridge.

"The Gospel hasn't failed in America, it just hasn't been tried," Kennedy says. "We have found that 75 per cent of those whom we visit in the home have never heard the Gospel of Christ.

"The church is losing the battle because most of its army is **AWOL. A few pastors are not going to scare the enemy. Ninety-five per cent of all church members have never led a person to Christ. Our job as pastors is to get the laymen back into the battle, equipped to do the work of ministry."**

James Kennedy does not browbeat his congregation into evangelizing. A visitor recently asked him after the morning worship service, "Where do you stand on evangelism? Are you doing anything?" The reply might be paraphrased from the inscription placed in St. Paul's Cathedral, London, by the son of architect Sir Christopher Wren: "If you would see where Coral Ridge stands on evangelism, look around you."

Calvary Temple

3

CALVARY TEMPLE
CHARLES E BLAIR PASTOR
CALVARY TEMPLE
CHARLES E BLAIR PASTOR

3

Calvary Temple

Denver, Colorado

At 1:58 a.m. a college student parks his car in a church lot in Denver, Colorado, and enters by a lighted doorway. A moment later a businessman arrives. At 2:00 a.m. they proceed into a side room to take the places of two women who have been praying there for the past hour. A night watchman sees the women safely to their cars.

Hour after hour throughout the week they come and go, these faithful links in a 24-hour prayer chain at Calvary Temple, an interdenominational church in the heart of Denver.

On a snowy Easter Sunday in March of 1970, I joined some 10,800 worshipers who attended Calvary Temple services. "I do not tell you that I can *explain* Easter," Pastor Charles Blair said to us from the pulpit, "but each of us can *experience* Easter." Even the 242 little tots in the church's six nursery departments that morning seemed to experience something of Easter beyond baby chicks. Perhaps they sensed the love in this church, expressed by a simple hand-lettered motto on a chalkboard in the Sunday School primary department: "Those who know Jesus best love him most."

At 11 a.m. Calvary's lovely brick and sandstone sanctuary became a television studio, as it has each Sunday since 1964. Audience ratings indicate that half of all TV sets turned on at 11 a.m. on Sunday in the Denver metropolitan area are tuned to Calvary Temple. And that is not all. Eight other stations throughout the "Rocky Mountain empire" carry the Calvary Temple service, swelling the congregation to 100,000 people.

Charles Blair has pastored Calvary Temple from its start in 1947. During this time the church has given $2 million to spread Christ's message throughout the world. In 1969 membership grew to 4,300 persons, and more than five hundred men and women, boys and girls were baptized. The Sunday School, with an average attendance of 2,650 pupils, is the tenth largest in the United States. **Assisting Blair is a team of eight pastors and a full time staff of more than forty-five employees, including custodial help — and a 360-20 IBM computer!**

Charles Blair was born into a family of Methodist background in Hiawatha, Kansas, in 1920, and grew to young manhood in Enid, Oklahoma. His parents were "good people of the soil. We never went to church, because we were too poor," he says. One day while selling *Collier's* and *Liberty* magazines he came upon a community church where he heard the Gospel and became a sincere believer in Christ. "Through my new birth experience my folks truly came to know the Lord."

Blair took a job at the J. C. Penney store in Enid. Encouraged toward further study by the store manager, he entered college. When funds ran out he withdrew from school and began to "preach wherever the Lord opened the door." He received ordination to the ministry in 1942. One day while conducting a revival meeting in McCook, Nebraska, he met an attractive young brunette pianist, Miss Betty Ruppert. They were married in 1943.

The Blairs were in Edinburgh, Scotland, on a preaching mission, when Denver's Central Assembly cabled him and invited him to become its pastor. He preached his first sermon there on June 22, 1947, after which the church's 32 members issued him a call. He accepted.

"The first year as pastor was a floundering experience," Blair recalls. "The turning point came when I read a book of sermons by Robert G. Lee, then pastor of Bellevue Baptist Church, Memphis, Tennessee. After reading that book I went to Memphis to interview Dr. Lee. For a week I trailed him everywhere he went. He paid 60 pastoral visits, and I said to him one day, 'Dr. Lee, if I made that many calls, I might have a big church too.' He replied, 'Well, why don't you?'

"Then I wrote to Dr. Louis Evans, pastor of Hollywood Presbyterian Church, and later I went to see him. He could spare me only twenty minutes, but they changed the course of my study life. 'Son,' Dr. Evans said, 'for every minute I preach, I study an hour.' Then he introduced me to Miss Henrietta Mears and from her I learned the value of Christian education. When I came back, Denver looked different to me.'

The church adopted a new constitution, taking the name Calvary Temple. Its bylaws provided that the young church would contribute a third of its annual income to missions. In 1947 the church gave $892 to missions; in 1969 it gave $336,986.

Blair's practical approach to the work of God's Kingdom soon led him to propose a church radio ministry. The deacons were unconvinced, but when the minister offered to back it with his own savings, they gave their approval. For the next eight years Charles and Betty Blair broadcast "Prayertime" to Denver listeners, and then for three years he was executive vice president and guest speaker on the daily "Haven of Rest." Today Pastor Blair is heard over radio KLIR five mornings a week in a popular half-hour "Counsel and Comment" program.

"There have been some important turning points in the life of Calvary Temple," says Pastor Blair. "One was the church's willingness to acquire ten acres of land in 1954. Our building seated only 420 people and we could not qualify for any kind of conventional financing, so we sold bonds. God allowed us to buy the property on which the State of Colorado had intended to build its Governor's mansion.

"Another step of faith was our decision to purchase an additional 46 acres in 1964. The Lord has not fully revealed to us his purpose for that land. A third step is the building of Life Center. The credit for this achievement goes to God. We are grateful for our board of 45 deacons and our people for being willing to take these steps of faith and, when the going has become rough, to pray and not to criticize."

Members of Calvary Temple believe Charles Blair is God's man for this hour. Oval Whitaker, a 64-year-old machinist who joined the congregation in 1948, is convinced that God's blessing is on Calvary Temple because of *right leadership* and the *priority of mission*. He says, "Pastor Blair's dedication has drawn good people to the work."

Among the "good people" are the eight assisting pastors, four full time children's division leaders, the director of development, Mr. Wendell Nance, and the business administrator, Mr. Roy Hudgins. The latter two are key men in programming the church's present and future.

Directing the nursery, pre-school, primary and junior divisions, respectively, in Christian education are Mrs. Joan Stevens, Mrs. Vernie Schorr, Miss Sharon Leach and Mrs. Yvonne Turkelson. Reverend Dave Koser pastors junior high young people and coordinates the church's weekday athletic and social activities.

Ministering to the high school and college young people is Pastor Jack McCahan. Two comfortable homes adjacent to the church parking lot — Omega House for high schoolers, Delta House for collegians — provide a facility for the church's ministry to the teen-agers and to 150,000 young Denverites who are in one of the colleges or universities, in military service or in business.

Pastors Irv Greaves and Orval Terrell are responsible for church ministries to adults, a challenging task in the Mile High City where adults average 12.2 years of formal education, second only to Washington, D.C. Reverend Clare Scratch, missionary for many years in China and India, dean of the pastoral staff, came from Canada last February to become the minister of visitation.

Like every metropolis, Denver has its poor. Calvary Temple's pastor of community outreach, Reverend Wally Early, is involved in a special ministry among these people. Persons of all races are welcome at Calvary Temple. At Mr. Early's disposal are the church's green-and-white buses that bring 200 children to the Sunday School each Lord's Day. Calvary Temple has shared in the financial support of churches in Denver's Negro and Spanish-speaking neighborhoods and has helped to bring the city's Calvary Indian Church to self-sustaining stature in 1969.

Working closely with these pastors and divisional directors is the minister of education, the Reverend James Spillman, a creative leader who, before coming to Calvary Temple in 1967, wrote the successful Omega curriculum for high school Christian education.

"Concept 5" produces much excitement among the lower grades in the Sunday School. "Simply put," Spillman says, "it is a three-hour educational period on Sunday morning involving five areas of Christian education (Bible study, missionary study, worship, physical expression and instruction). It employs flexible modular scheduling, individual readiness testing and a low student/teacher ratio, using a specialized staff."

Primary Sunday School workers were drilled for four months before becoming the first to experiment with Concept 5. The primaries moved into a 7,500 square-foot building on the church's

Christian education campus.

Calvary is a singing church. No fewer than nine graded choirs and three choral groups are making music for the Lord each week. Presiding at this feast of sound is the Reverend Harvey W. Schroeder, minister of music, who has more than 550 singers involved in his programs.

Calvary Temple shares in the support of 85 missionary families in 50 countries and has erected nine churches or chapels overseas, the latest one in a prisoner-of-war camp in Saigon, Vietnam. In 1969 the church sent Pastor Blair and a Russian-born linguist on a 28-day preaching mission to 15 cities in Russia. He preached in ten evangelical churches and shared dialogue with pastors in each city, while also serving as an emissary from Denver's Jews to the Jewish communities in Russia.

One Sunday morning in 1970, Blair preached on the Christian's responsibility to lead others to Jesus Christ. To illustrate, he introduced from the pulpit a Chinese shopkeeper, Mrs. Lily Chinn, who had come to Christ through the church's witness in 1963. Before the TV cameras were turned off, 27 of Mrs. Chinn's relatives, including her aged mother and father, all former Buddhists, stood with her, each having been brought to Christ through person-to-person evangelism.

Three years ago Calvary Temple commissioned an independent research company to poll the people of Denver and determine what questions were uppermost in their minds. From 5,000 responses this company listed the ten most frequently asked questions. Then Pastor Blair publicized a series of sermons he would deliver, dealing with these problems one by one. The public response to this series was so great that many times two evening services were required to accommodate the people.

Who is the man behind this amazing church? Roy Hudgins describes his pastor as a "great preacher and teacher." Charles Blair is also a hunter, an art collector, an author. But pre-eminently he is a pastor. "I don't know of any other job I'd rather have than to be a pastor," he confides, "because this is where the battle is raging. People have problems and they need a shepherd.

"I am as excited today as I was the day I came back from visiting Dr. Lee. It seems I have just unpacked. I have spent 20 years getting some facilities and building a staff. Now, if our Lord tarries we are really ready to give something to missions."

As a person, Blair is a man of goals and faith in God. Each

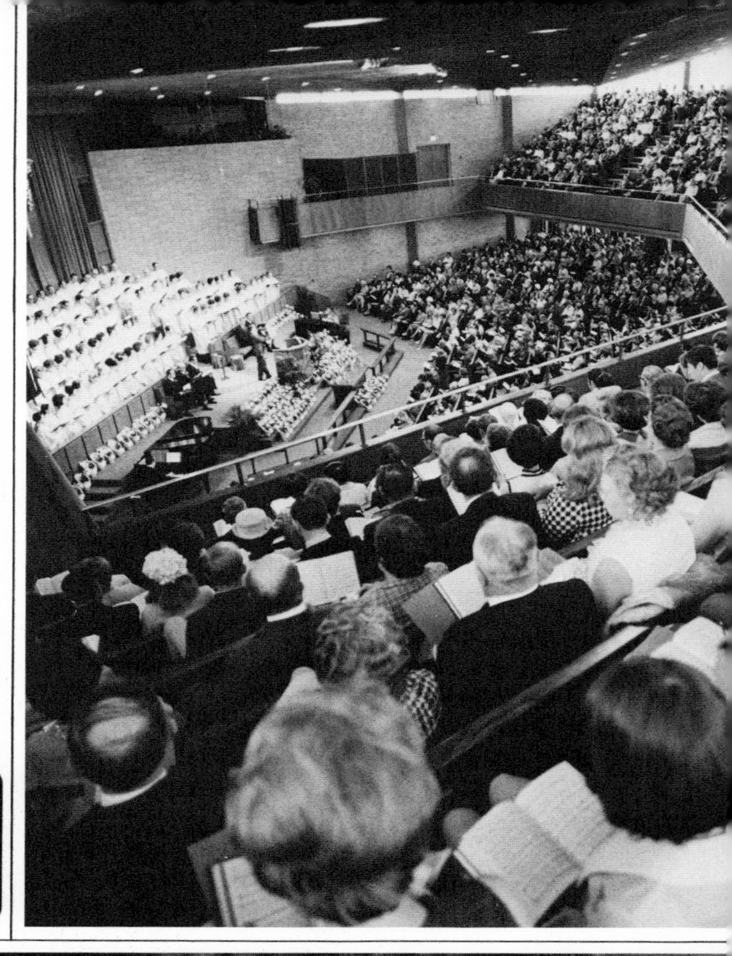

Calvary Temple is a busy and popular place on Sunday mornings. Pictured at left is senior pastor Charles E. Blair.

time he preaches he invites men to surrender their lives to Jesus Christ. "Through every age faith has been the test which God has placed on every man," he says. "It has always been required of man to believe that God, our heavenly Father, wants the very best for each of us. That is still the basis of God's dealing with us. Take the faith he has given you and direct it back to him and his promises, and watch it grow into a strong, mountain-moving faith."

First Baptist Church
Dallas

'4

THLAND LIFE

4

First Baptist Church

Dallas, Texas

At high noon in the dignified old auditorium of the First Baptist Church of Dallas, Texas, the Sunday worship hour is drawing to a close. Through the gentle rustle one can feel the strongly beating pulse of this downtown church. A full house of 2,600 worshipers gives quiet attention to the summation of the message from God's Word. Here and there a head is bowed in prayer. Most of the congregation keep their eyes riveted on the rock-jawed prophet of a pastor, Dr. W. Amos Criswell, who is speaking about "Do or Die Decisions."

"Any ultimate decision that changes life is centered on God," he says. "If it's not centered on God it is peripheral. If you have a faith in God, it will be tested. Welcome that trial. If you don't have that faith in God, make that decision in your heart where you are. On the first note of the first stanza of the song, stand up coming. Do it now."

They come. A young couple from Arlington, Texas. A youth to profess his faith in Jesus Christ. *I have decided to follow Jesus,* sings the choir. From the choir steps a mother. "Pastor, the sermon was for me," she says brokenly. "I've been asking why. Now I see the Lord is only putting my faith to the test." *All to Jesus I surrender.* A family comes. A girl from Kansas. A mother and her two daughters. An assistant pastor prays with each one. A couple from Louisiana wants to join the church. *Have Thine own way, Lord.*

No one is now extending the appeal for decisions; no man, that is. When they have ceased to come, the congregation is seated. One by one Dr. Criswell introduces those who have come forward, and for those inquirers who wish to become members of First Baptist a vote is taken.

As I sat in a pew reflecting on my own childhood in this church, I could see a pulpit prince of another generation, Dr. George W. Truett, calling men to the Savior. For 47 years until his death in 1944 he had served First Church, and had become a leader so beloved the world over that to this day his sermons are broadcast on radio in Dallas each Sunday. As he would look out upon the expanse of the Sunday evening congregation at the close of the baptismal service, Dr. Truett would say, "Yet there is room." Today his successor is leading the church to provide "yet more room" for ministries to a congregation approaching 16,000 members.

The imposing Gothic sanctuary erected in 1890 stands catercornered from the site on which the church built its original frame structure in 1873. First Baptist now owns that plot of land and the five-story parking facility standing upon it. It owns two more city blocks which house 23 floors of educational space, each arranged for departmental and classroom use; a parking structure, a roller rink, bowling lanes and a full-sized gymnasium. The church still must rent a floor of the Cotton Exchange Building and three rooms in the downtown YMCA for some of the adult Sunday School classes. "People ask us how we keep the swimming pool from leaking," says the Reverend Dan Beam, minister of recreation. "That is one thing we don't have!"

In 1970 the church launched its most ambitious building project, one that will provide four more floors of educational space, double the parking and recreational facilities, and house a 2,500-seat dining hall that can serve as an "interim auditorium" when the present sanctuary building must be replaced.

"We seek to make First Church the center of life for your whole family," Assistant Pastor Melvin R. Carter tells new members. This explains why expansion has been the pattern since Criswell became pastor 26 years ago. In his first sermon to the church he said, "We'll go on and up with our various works. We'll give to missions more than ever before. We'll have a Sunday School with 5,000 pupils coming every week."

Average attendance at Sunday School for the first half of 1970 was 5,282 people. With the $1-million mission funds in its $2.4-million budget for 1970, the First Baptist Church is bringing hope and spiritual help to people all over the free world. Six local missions, four situated in disadvantaged areas of "Big D," extend the influence of this great seeking church into every nook and cranny of metropolitan Dallas (population 1,430,500). One pastor conducts an urban ministry to underprivileged in the Good Shepherd Department; another is pastor to "Silent Friends," deaf folk who are an object of special church care.

The church was slow to welcome black Christians into its fellowship. Dr. Criswell's segregationist views received wide publicity during the '50s. As he explains in *Look Up, Brother!* (his latest book), "I came to the profound conclusion that to separate by coercion the body of Christ on the basis of skin pigmentation was unthinkable, unchristian, and unacceptable to God." In 1968 he unburdened his heart to the 200-member board of deacons and after considerable deliberation the deacons voted unanimously to declare publicly that First Baptist is a "church of the open door."

Reared in a devout home in Texline, in the northwestern corner of Texas, Criswell knew when he was but six years old that he wanted to be a preacher some day. The following year, 1919, he went forward in a revival meeting and professed his faith in Christ. After graduating from Amarillo High School he was licensed to preach at age 17 and entered Baylor University in Waco. He first pastored the Baptist church in Devil's Bend, and later in Pulltight, near Waco.

An accomplished debater and trombone player, Criswell graduated from Baylor with high honors in English and proceeded to Southern Baptist Theological Seminary in 1931 to earn his master's and doctor's degrees (Ph.D. in New Testament interpretation).

At the Baptist church in Mount Washington, Kentucky, where he served briefly as part-time pastor, he met the girl who was to share his life. Miss Betty Marie Harris was a student at Kentucky State College and the church pianist. They were married in 1935. From seminary he was called to pastorates in Chickasha and Muskogee, Oklahoma, and to Dallas in October, 1944, to fill the pulpit left vacant by Dr. Truett's homegoing.

"When I first began preparing for my life work," says Criswell, "I asked the Lord to help me preach without notes. It frightened

The largest Baptist church in the world is built upon and dedicated to the teaching of the Scripture. Here may be seen the congregation at worship, a response to the invitation, an adult training class. Fulcrum of the church's busy life is committed staff headed by Dr. W. Amos Criswell.

me to death, but I trusted him for it." He delivers his carefully crafted expository messages today to a TV audience of 125,000 viewers every Sunday. Both early morning and evening Sunday services are broadcast by radio in Dallas.

"I discovered at Muskogee that people want to hear the Bible," he continued. "Shortly after I arrived in Dallas, a retired preacher told me that I would save myself a lot of trouble if I would preach through the Scriptures, and that is what I did. For 17 years and eight months I preached from Genesis to Revelation, chapter by chapter. The people were blessed by it and I cannot tell you how my own soul grew."

It takes more than preaching says Dr. Criswell, to establish a church. He has attracted some of the best qualified men and women in his denomination to develop an effective Christian education program and to direct a closely graded, warmly evangelistic Sunday School. While the church has taken steps to enlarge its facilities, Dr. Criswell remains the sometimes-weeping, sometimes-shouting revival preacher, holding meetings South and North, and — (in recent years) — all over the world as president of the Southern Baptist Convention (1968-1970). He also conducts pre-Easter noonday services in Dallas' Palace Theater, a popular tradition inaugurated by Dr. Truett in 1917.

"For a good many years I have wanted a school that would teach the Bible to young preachers," he told me. "I believe that when God puts something in your heart he wants you to do, he will confirm it by an outward sign. During the week after I shared my plan for such a school with my congregation, Dr. T. A. Patterson, executive secretary of the Texas Convention, told me that of the 4,500 Southern Baptist pastors in Texas, only 800 of them have a seminary degree. Next winter (1970) we will initiate the first semester of our Baptist Bible Institute. It will include evening courses in Hebrew and Greek, theology, old and New Testament, Church history and evangelism. Distinguished professors of the Bible who are members of our church will form the teaching faculty."

First Church already has a sizable school for "young prophets" going full blast. More than a thousand children attend Sunday School and 1,142 young people study the Bible in small classes in the junior- and senior-high divisions, 542 of them in a thorough "high school accredited Bible course" taught by some of the church's ablest teachers.

Under Robert H. Coleman's direction during the Truett era, First Baptist became a great singing church. Today the choirs set a musical feast before the congregation 52 Sundays a year, and especially during the Christmas and Easter seasons, and also when the Chapel Choir climaxes its summer tour with concerts in the home church. One hundred eighty high schoolers and college freshmen and sophomores have just completed an Orient choir tour during which they sang in Japanese and Thai as well as in their own tongue. "Singing in this choir has revolutionized these young people," says Donald R. Porter, a banker who with his wife has accompanied the Chapel Choir as a sponsor for six years.

The music ministry, under the leadership of Lee Roy Till, fits squarely within an educational context. Till believes "there is an inner value for every person who participates in music." He and his assistant, Perry Taylor, are providing a musical outlet in the Lord's service for everyone from age four through adult life who wants to become involved.

Texans have a proverbial reputation for doing things in a big way. At First Church we find midweek teachers' and workers' meetings, the "Harvest Couples," the Fishermen's Club, the day nursery, summer camp, special ministries to the oral deaf and the mentally retarded, to professional groups such as physicians and dentists, to Oriental and Latin ethnic communities — all of these emanating from a spirit of brotherly love and evangelistic concern.

When a high school Sunday School department held an all-night party in the recreation building, a half dozen of the young people were led to Christ.

"What has made us strong is standing firm in teaching the Word of God," says Miss Millie Kohn, who has directed the church's junior work for 19 years. The congregation expends unlimited effort to bring people to church, where they can hear the Bible taught. Statistics are the easiest thing to obtain in a Southern Baptist church. According to records of the Sunday School, church members, excluding all staff personnel, make an average total of 45 contacts a day in Dallas County on the King's business.

One day Dr. Criswell stopped at a coin collector's store near the barber shop he patronizes. He made repeated attempts to become acquainted with the owner, to learn about his trade and to win his friendship. Eventually the pastor had an opportunity to talk to him about God, and today the man and his family are a part of the congregation of this downtown lighthouse.

In the centennial (1868-1968) volume, *The First Baptist Church of Dallas,* Dr. Leon McBeth comments on Criswell's "unique ability to speak the language [of the youngsters] and to establish rapport with them. Every child who joins the church first has a personal conference with the pastor in his office. They talk about the meaning of conversion and baptism, and the skilful pastor leads the child to discuss his own personal religious experience. Then they kneel and pray together." No child under nine years of age is baptized.

Dr. Billy Graham, a member of First Church since 1953, says of Criswell, "The open Bible in his hand is more than decoration. He explains it and proclaims it. The Word of God comes alive."

What will become of this giant city church when Criswell is gone? To answer that question, the pastor reaches back to the opening message of his ministry at First Baptist in 1944, which carried a memorable quotation from Dr. Truett: "God buries the workman, but the work goes on." Dr. Criswell believes that the ministry of First Church to the people of Dallas has been built upon the Lord God and that God cannot fail. As his favorite Scripture expresses it, "The grass withereth, the flower fadeth: but the word of our God shall stand forever."

Park Street Congregational Church

5

BOSTON
COMMON
THIS IS YOUR PARK
KEEP IT CLEAN
BOARD OF PARK COMMISSIONERS

5

Park Street Congregational Church

Boston, Massachusetts

Aspiration: the delicate lines of a white Christopher Wren church spire.

Certitude: the strong and stately brick frame of a commodious meetinghouse.

Such is the blend God used to form Park Street Congregational Church of Boston, Massachusetts. The hope has been man's through 161 years of history. The certitude has been — God in the midst.

Each day during the summer a thousand visitors follow Boston's Freedom Trail from the Common through the State House to Park Street Church to learn some of its secrets. They find that "Brimstone Corner" took its name, not from the pulpit, but from the cellar. There brimstone for gunpowder was stored during the War of 1812. They learn, among other things, that the American Temperance Society originated in the church vestry in 1826; that William Lloyd Garrison delivered his first anti-slavery speech from this pulpit on July 4, 1829; that "America" was sung in public here for the first time on July 4, 1831.

On Sundays many of these tourists return and join regular worshipers in mounting the broad stone steps of the church to hear God's secrets explained. Amid all the cross-currents of New England theology, Park Street Church has remained a bastion of evangelical faith and missionary outreach. Today the congregation numbers 2,338 members. For 32 years the church grew and prospered under the watch-care of a man who has perhaps exerted as much influence upon the evangelical churches of America as any other individual: Dr. Harold John Ockenga.

"It is not the architecture of the church that makes Park Street famous," said Dr. Ockenga in 1968. "It is not because of the many historical events which have occurred in connection with the church. It is not the series of revivals that have taken place, beginning in 1823 and continuing to 1964, under men like Charles Finney, D. L. Moody, Billy Sunday, J. Wilbur Chapman, Billy Graham. It is not our orthodox commitment, which stemmed the tide of Unitarianism and gave rebirth to Trinitarianism in New England.

"Park Street Church is best known because of its missionary program and interest."* With the commissioning of the first missionaries to the Sandwich Islands (now known as Hawaii) in 1819, the church began its amazing overseas outreach which has continued to the present time.

The Rev. Paul Elmer Toms, whom the Park Street congregation sent to Hawaii in missionary service in 1952, became its fourteenth pastor in 1969. The church is affiliated with The Conservative Congregational Christian Conference.

This historic house of worship was born in 1809 out of "concerts of prayer" that had been carried on for six years. On January 10, 1810, in dedicating their first building, Dr. Edward Dorr Griffin prophesied, "Should this church stand a century and a half, and its seats be generally filled, how many thousands will hear the Gospel within these walls! Millions of times will all those thousands look back from eternity to this house, with inconceivable pleasure or pain. . . . " Griffin served as the church's first pastor from 1811 to 1815.

In the first 33 years of its life, 70 members of Park Street Church went out under God's blessing to help form seven orthodox Congregational churches in Boston. But by 1900 many members had moved to the suburbs — often leaving "pew taxes" unpaid. The church roll dropped below the 400 mark.

At last, under the ministry of Arcturus Z. Conrad, pastor from 1905-1937, Park Street began to flourish. The weekly broadcast he inaugurated in 1923 continues today as "The Radio Pulpit of New England." Boston stations WEZE and WCOP carry morning and evening messages to six states and eastern Canada.

Harold Ockenga was 31 years old when Dr. Conrad asked him to leave his Presbyterian pulpit in Pittsburgh, Pennsylvania, and

"Brimstone Corner," by H. Crosby Englizian (© 1968, Moody Press), provided background material for this article

become his assistant in November, 1936. Upon Conrad's death the following year Park Street Church called Ockenga as pastor. Trained at Taylor University and Westminster Theological Seminary, Ockenga received his Ph.D. degree from the University of Pittsburgh in 1939. As Miss Marion Clark, his secretary during the early years of his pastorate, puts it, "He's Dutch. When he gets an idea, he goes to it."

For building the church, Ockenga specified four foundation pillars. First and most important is the establishing work of the Holy Spirit. The other pillars are world missions, evangelism, and Christian education of the whole man. He instituted an annual missionary conference in 1940 and for six years Dr. Oswald J. Smith, pastor of The Peoples Church, Toronto, directed it. During the period 1944 to 1969 the annual missionary budget rose from $45,000 to $344,000. In 1969, 90 missionaries, serving in 44 nations, including Canada and the United States, were fully supported by gifts from the Park Street Church. They engaged in such varied ministries as medical work, Bible translation, Gospel broadcasting, church-planting, literature distribution, elementary education and Bible-school training. In Mexico, to take one example, the church played a leading role in establishing the Tarascan Missionary Society, now laboring among Indians in Michoacan, Mexico.

The annual ten-day missionary conference serves to bring the spiritual needs of a world before the congregation and to harness its energies for the Gospel. Representatives of evangelical mission agencies mingle with the Park Street people to bring up-to-the-minute reports from their fields. One entire day is given to intercessory prayer. As the conference closes members bring their gifts and pledges, and pre-schoolers come with tin cans filled with pennies and nickels they have been saving all year.

Every three years, prior to the conference, a contingent of the church's high school young people spend two weeks on the field with one of the church's missionaries. The Reverend Sherwood Strodel led his fourth tour in April, 1970, accompanying 16 high schoolers to Mexico City, where they observed the work of and completed a field project with Dr. and Mrs. Dow Robinson, linguists with the Wycliffe Bible Translators.

When the church's permit to preach on the famed Boston Common was revoked in 1945, circumstances led to the creation of the "Mayflower pulpit." Charles Dooley, owner of the Mayflower Hotels on Cape Cod, had found Christ under the influence

While retaining its traditional beauty the church on "Brimstone Corner" adapts to the life style of today. Top center, is Pastor Toms. Upper left, a youth Bible study.

PARK STREET CHURCH

of Dr. Ockenga's preaching shortly after the revocation. Dooley offered to build a balcony pulpit on the front exterior wall facing the Common. Since 1946 Park Street's ministers have evangelized from that pulpit each Sunday night during the summer.

The church's vision did not overlook what is perhaps the greatest mission field on the church's doorstep: the 100,000 college and university students of the Greater Boston area. In 1948 the church called its first full-time minister to students. The Reverend Wayne Anderson, a graduate of Fuller Theological Seminary, presently serves in that capacity.

On Sundays after the evening service some one hundred of these collegians gather for a "Break Out" on one of the campuses. In songs that are fast-moving and contemporary they recall God's work in the past, and tell of their response as committed members of Christ's body. From the approximately forty collegians who are becoming "team" members, some spontaneously talk about new insights they have received the previous week from the Scriptures. "You can feel the love of the body of Christ at Park Street Church," says Chuck White, a Harvard senior. Mrs. "Ginny" Smedberg, a graduate of Smith College and a Park Street missionary to students, directs the church's work among girl students.

"As young people find their own needs being met in the fellowship of believers," says Anderson, "they reach out to other people and bring them under the sound of the Gospel so that they can respond to Christ. Park Street is obviously a symbol of the social order at a time when the church is being challenged, maligned and ripped apart; and our college students are learning what it means to be committed to the church as the expression of Christ in the world. During the fantastic polarization on campus last year many of them were engaged in a useful ministry of reconciliation." Regular Bible classes are led by Collegiate Club members at Harvard, Boston University, Wellesley and Gordon.

"Graduate students and other young professionals who desire to be integrally involved in active obedience to Jesus Christ" (so reads the statement of purpose) make up the "Grad Group." These single men and women are demonstrating to the world that missions is not limited to something "overseas," in another language. Some 125 young adults participate in 18 action groups which meet for Bible study and discussion. The "Grad Group" also hosts international students, and ministers to shut-ins and elderly people. Some are engaged in tutoring residents of Boston's ghettos; others help raise scholarships for black students. Another group works among alcoholics and "unemployables."

In the midst of Park Street's expansion program in 1969, Dr. Toms informed his congregation that the Twelfth Street Baptist Church in Boston's black community was renovating its building. He asked for help. The next Sunday a gift of $14,000 was presented to the Negro congregation.

Dr. Toms, a graduate of Bob Jones University, was a student at Fuller Seminary when he met Dr. Ockenga, then president of Fuller as well as pastor of Park Street. Fresh from a visit to Hawaii, in 1952 Ockenga offered the Washington-born seminary senior the support of the Park Street Church if he and his wife, Eva, would serve as missionaries in Hawaii. Toms said he would go. For five years he was engaged in evangelistic work on the Kona Coast of Hawaii, and served five more years as pastor of the Haili Congregational Church in Hilo; then he went to Sydney, Australia, at the request of the Congregational churches there, to lead them in evangelism. In 1965 he returned to the staff of Park Street Church.

When Dr. Ockenga announced his resignation in 1968 many of his church folk did not take him seriously. But his decision was final, and the congregation turned to Paul Toms, whom it had learned to love during the four years he had counseled and visited as the assistant pastor. In the same month that Gordon Divinity School conferred on him the honorary degree of doctor of divinity, Paul Toms was called to the Park Street pulpit. Deacon "Ted" Lindsay, an engineer, sums up the affection the congregation feels for Toms: "He had a pair of shoes to fill, but he couldn't be more Biblical. He's right on the beam."

From Cartagena, Colombia, came a letter to the DECISION office, recommending "one of the greatest churches in all the world today — Park Street Church." The writer, Miss Muriel Clement, serving with the Latin America Mission, went on: "It was in this church that I received my call from Jesus Christ to be a missionary, and for 18 years this church has fully supported me with gifts and prayers."

This willingness to take seriously the instructions concerning "the Great Commission," as Dr. Toms tells it, has made the impact and the honored name of the church on Brimstone Corner known around the world.

First United Methodist Church

6

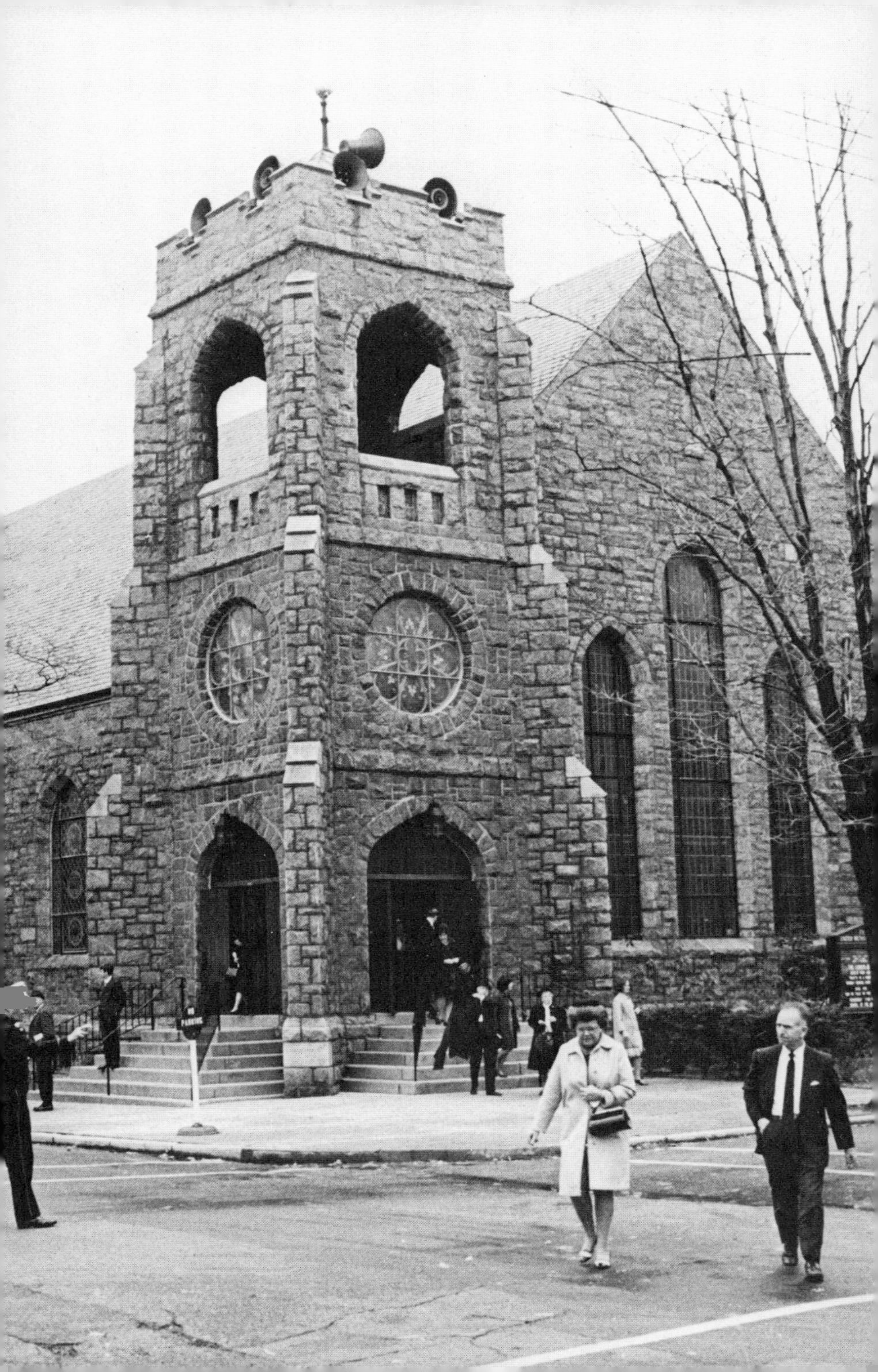

6

First United Methodist Church

Collingswood, New Jersey

When the poet Walt Whitman retired to his "modest little cottage" in Camden, New Jersey, in 1884, the suburb of Collingswood was just getting its start. Wooden walks connected the post office with the three stores and the one-room schoolhouse. A dozen kerosene street lamps held their evening rendezvous with the lamplighter, except when there was a full moon. For their nightly protection the 200 residents paid 25¢ a week per family to the town watchmen.

Two years later nine of the local citizens met with the presiding elder of the Camden District of the Methodist Episcopal Church to organize a congregation. During the course of the evening one William Collings rose and said that he wished to become a Christian. *Even before this new church was born it was reconciling souls to God.* In two months the First Methodist Church of Collingswood conducted its first public worship, and Danny Green, preacher of the Gospel by vocation and paperhanger by avocation, spoke from the text: "My God shall supply all your need" (Philippians 4:19).

The first Methodist missionaries from England sent out by John Wesley (Joseph Pilmore and Richard Boardman) disembarked in 1769 from the *Mary and Elizabeth* at Gloucester Point, just three miles from the present site of First Church. Today Collingswood (named after the Collings family) is a lovely tree-lined borough of 17,370 people. Nestled in its residential area like a mother hen, First Church seeks to remind 20th-century urbanized man that God is *here.* The Reverend Philip Everett Worth is the senior minister.

A casual glance around the narthex of First Church reveals the far-ranging interests of an energetic congregation. Letters are displayed from missionaries and national Christians in such distant places as India, Alaska, the Niger Republic, Brazil. On a wall plaque which reads "Christian Service Fellowship" appear names of 109 sons and daughters of the church who have gone out as ministers during the church's 85-year history.

Who are the Collingswood 109? A number of them are Methodist pastors and ministers' wives serving in the Southern New Jersey Conference and other conferences in the United States. One was Vincent J. Joy, late founder of Central Alaskan Missions, which today operates Alaska Bible College with 40 students, Faith Hospital, and a radio station in Glennallen, Alaska. Another is Mrs. Ruth Crawford Porter, whose late husband, Percy Crawford, was founder and president of King's College and Pinebrook Bible Conference. She was one of five Duvall children who were nurtured in First Church and entered Christian service.

Another is Newton Kapp, veteran missionary in the Niger Republic under the Sudan Interior Mission. Kapp, a young Armenian immigrant boarding in Collingswood when the church's building was gutted by fire in April, 1932, was challenged by the courage of the church people as they rallied to rebuild in the depth of a nationwide depression. All that he had to give was his carfare, but he did that, and for several months he walked daily the 15-mile round trip from Collingswood over the Ben Franklin Bridge to school in Philadelphia.

The church seeks to maintain a climate that will produce Christian workers. "Around here a kid who declares for Christ and Christian service is a hero," says "Gus" Gilbert, news bureau manager for a transportation company and chairman of the church's commission on education. Last year 15 teen-agers spent the Christmas holidays on projects with missionaries in Haiti. Through such activities as the fall missionary conference, youth weekends and the Fellowship of the Yoke, the call of God to carry out the Great Commission is kept before the people. "Jesus said," explains Worth, "'Take my yoke upon you, and learn of me.' Through the Fellowship we encourage our people to discover the nature of the ministry the Lord has for them."

That this awareness is fostered among young and old alike is apparent from observing the family of Jerry Richards. An engineer, Jerry became number 109 in the Christian Service Fellowship when he moved to Waxhaw, North Carolina, headquarters of Jungle Aviation and Radio Service (JAARS is the air and radio arm of Wycliffe Bible Translators). This widower is investing a lifetime of electronic experience in obedience to what he believes is God's will. His two daughters and their husbands are also Wycliffe missionaries.

Not listed in the Christian Service Fellowship are the 1,335 present members whom Pastor Worth counts on as full-time ministers as well. For instance, there is a senior Coed at Rutgers University in Camden, who attends the 8:30 a.m. worship service so that she may teach young people and play the piano for a small Methodist church 20 minutes away in south Philadelphia. Three young men — a Hallmark salesman, a tenth-grade English teacher, and a Faith Seminary student serving as a pastoral intern — direct a Saturday "cager" program in the church gymnasium, bumping elbows with 80 junior and senior high boys.

And there is Frances Casperson. "Fran" is the wife of George Casperson, a corporation executive. Their home has been jovially tagged the "Casperson Evangelistic Center" by their son-in-law, Ted, who considers them one of two human factors that brought him to Christ. "The other influence," Ted adds, "was the people of First Church." Mrs. Casperson teaches a ladies' Sunday School class, but her heart these days is in neighboring Camden, south Jersey's center of commerce and industry, opposite Philadelphia on the Delaware River.

When fire destroyed the Trinity Methodist Church of Camden in 1965, its small congregation needed help. First Church had already given birth to four new Methodist Churches in the area, and required all its workers to care for its own outreach and growing responsibilities. However, the Caspersons joined a few lay people in their congregation and lent a hand in Camden. With some Trinity folk they organized weekday Bible classes in a nearby Pentecostal church. Mrs. Casperson began knocking on doors, telling the black, Puerto Rican and white parents about their children. "When the people saw that we really cared and were not just do-gooders, they began to accept us," she says.

In 1969 Fellowship House on Camden's Broadway was opened. Some sixty members of First Church have renovated an old two-story house, furnishing it from their attics, and now they conduct

Through traditional services, the Cagers, Fellowship House and many other outlets, First United Methodist touches its community for Christ. Pictured at lower right is Reverend Philip Worth.

CAGERS

a through-the-week program which includes Bible classes, clubs, tutoring, baby-sitting and home nursing services. Clothes, donated textbooks, and Christian literature are going into children's hands. The church hopes to engage a couple to direct a full time program in the House and begin worship services.

When Dr. Frank Bateman Stanger resigned the Collingswood pastorate to become president of Asbury Theological Seminary in 1959, the church's administrative board requested the bishop to appoint Philip Worth to be the pastor. He had been minister of the Mount Hope Methodist Church of Media, Pennsylvania, which grew under his leadership from 200 members to 1,200.

"The adult department of the Sunday School," says Worth, "comprised half of the enrolment of the school when my wife, Dorothy, and I came to First Church. Fifty per cent of the adults were 65 and older. No new homes were being built in Collingswood. I wondered what to expect. As it has turned out, we are drawing young families from as far away as 15 miles. Since we are only ten minutes by the Hi-Speed Line from downtown Philadelphia we always have a number of students and young business people involved in our church life."

Sunday School attendance averages 550 pupils. In addition, 85 ladies attend Mrs. Worth's weekly Bible class and 150 persons are present at the two-hour mid-week Bible study. Many local residents learn of First Church through its Sunday morning broadcast over WTMR.

For a dozen or more college and career young people, Sunday dinner with the pastor and his wife is more important than almost any other date of the week. "It's like they've adopted us," says "Andy" Michael, one college girl. In the summer of 1970 being trained by the youth director, Wayne G. Schoonmaker, and Roland Mitcheson of Ambassadors for Christ International, the high school young people opened "The Way Out," a coffee house for Collingswood youth. Fifteen decisions for Christ were registered in ten nights. Local police were so impressed that they tried to persuade First Church to make the coffee house permanent.

Pastor and Mrs. Worth have begun a ministry among a "Leisure Time" group, church members of retirement age. A third of the First Church congregation are senior citizens, some of whom live in the Methodist Home for the Aged in Collingswood, which is linked by telephone relay with the services in the sanctuary. Each month Leisure Timers enjoy dinner together at the church, and occasionally they take a short tour of scenic and historic sites. One of those in the group on a recent outing was a lonely Jewish widow. After she heard Bob Roland, one of three pastoral interns serving the church, lead morning meditations in the book of Romans, she exclaimed, "I have never heard such teaching. And now that I have friends, I wouldn't miss Leisure Time for anything."

First Church has never held a fund-raising meeting for its own finances. The granite-walled facilities, valued at $1.5 million, are debt free, enabling the congregation to give $50,000 annually to missions.

"Many churches consider holding the line on attendance to be a sort of victory today," states Worth, "but we are growing and moving ahead. Methodist churches of evangelical persuasion are not experiencing the decline in attendance and finances that has affected so many congregations of the traditional denominations in the last few years."

In 1966 the Reverend Charles W. Keysor, pastor of the Grace United Methodist Church of Elgin, Illinois, called on evangelical Methodists to organize within their denomination. He asked Worth to become the chairman of the board of directors of the new movement. Keysor founded a quarterly periodical, *Good News*, whose subscription list has grown to 11,000.

Good News sponsored a four-day Convocation of United Methodists for Evangelical Christianity in Dallas, Texas, and it drew more than 1,600 Methodist pastors and laymen from 48 states and four continents. "The response to *Good News* has gone far beyond our dreams and expectations," Worth says.

The Reverend Philip Worth was born a twin in Woodhaven, Long Island, in 1919. His twin brother died when he was 22 months old. Phil attended the 9,000-student Boys' High School in Brooklyn.

"For me as a teen-ager, church was dead and boring," he says. "My aunt had attended a meeting Jack Wyrtzen was holding in Woodhaven, and at her invitation our family went along the next Sunday. I was quite taken by it. On our third visit I was saved, and so were my mother, father and aunt. Our whole home was changed. It was just as Paul says in Acts: 'Believe on the Lord Jesus Christ, and thou shalt be saved, *and thy house.*' My father, a postal carrier, had been an alcoholic, but before long the alcohol went."

Worth had wanted to become a doctor, but the promptings of the Holy Spirit began to draw him into the Christian ministry. He became a member of Wyrtzen's first brass quartet, accompanying the evangelist on Gospel trips. One night he was asked to testify. A born stutterer, Worth felt it would be impossible, but when his turn came to speak he was able to relate clearly and directly what Christ meant to him.

After graduating from The King's College, Briarcliff Manor, New York, he completed studies at the Temple University School of Theology in Philadelphia and was ordained a minister of the Methodist Church.

"Phil Worth demonstrates the fruit of the Spirit," J. Robert Ellis says of his pastor. Ellis directs the five First Church choirs, and is training their first hand-bell choir. Sunday evenings at First Church the congregation lays aside its *Methodist Hymnal* to sing from the less formal *Crowning Glory Hymnal,* accompanied by an orchestra and led alternately by four lay song leaders. A 305-bell Schulmerich Carillon bell system, given as a memorial gift by a member of the church, adds great versatility to the pipe organ in worship services.

Pastor Worth's preaching is didactic, serial, current. He regularly expounds the books of the Bible, paying special attention to the prophetic Scriptures. "I don't see how any man can preach today without getting into prophecy," he says.

Once an eccentric young man intruded into a First Church ladies' gathering and told them, "I am Jesus Christ." Pastor Worth changed his topic for the following Sunday night, using the incident to illustrate a message on "Signs of Jesus' Coming Multiply." "The very first sign Jesus gave to his disciples to indicate his second advent," said Worth, "was 'For many shall come in my name, saying I am Christ.'"

On the infrequent occasions when he is away from the pulpit, he follows a rule given him by his seminary dean: "Always bring in a better speaker than yourself." Since 1955 the church has sat under many of the nation's leading evangelists and Bible teachers in its "Ten Summer Sunday Evenings" series. Three retired ministers on the staff do most of the pastoral visiting.

So the lamp of the Lord glows brightly at the First United Methodist Church, Collingswood. The people share the excitement of adventuring with God into the unknown, confident that "*their* God will supply all *their* need according to his riches in glory by Christ Jesus."

Garden Grove Community Church

7

7

Garden Grove Community Church

Garden Grove, California

The Santa Ana winds that sweep down the Sierra Madre Mountains and across the Los Angeles Basin have turned the peaceful chaparral country into a fiery holocaust more than once.

In recent years this populous region seems to have entered a season of another wind. The Spirit of God is blowing upon "dry reeds" in the youth subculture, burning his way through a drug-oriented society. In the heart of this "Jesus revolution" stands the Garden Grove Community Church, the largest congregation in California's Orange County. In 1955 it consisted of two members, the Reverend Robert Harold Schuller and his wife. Their arduous door-to-door canvass uncovered only two other families of their sponsoring denomination (The Reformed Church in America). Prospects for growth were dim.

Today Garden Grove Church is riding an incredible wave of expansion; its membership exceeded 6,000 persons early in 1971. Its "Tower of Hope" rises above all other structures in Orange County. It claims to be the largest walk-in, drive-in church in the world. Its Sunday color telecast ("The Hour of Power," KTLA Channel 5), viewed weekly by one million Californians, commands the highest rating of any regular religious program in the area. Its attractive buildings are situated on 20 acres of land near a freeway interchange.

To understand the Garden Grove Community Church, let's trace the path of one family, beginning with its initial contact with the church. Frank and Anne Phillips were actual members, though their names have been altered. When they moved from New Jersey to Anaheim, they thought they had discovered paradise. Minutes away by freeway were the beaches. Within easy driving distance were the mountains. Just down the street was Disneyland.

Soon after they had settled in the nation's fastest-growing county (Orange County's population: 1,409,335), Anne suspected that something was missing in her world. Although she had become a Christian as a child, she and Frank had not attended church regularly.

One Sunday morning in 1968 she drove by herself into the parking lot of the Garden Grove Church. As other cars parked alongside, an usher stepped to the car window and greeted her with a bulletin. He directed her attention to the announcement: "If you have a car radio, please turn to 540 on your dial for this service. If you do not have a radio, please park by the amplifiers in the back row."

Through the windshield Anne could see the spray from 12 fountains leaping from a shallow pond alongside the 250-foot clear glass wall of the sanctuary. Four bell towers, each a hundred feet high, silhouetted the skyline. A gleaming 14-story structure, topped by a 90-foot steel cross, rose alongside the bells.

Now Anne's attention returned to the "glass cathedral" before her. Two 25-foot sections of the sanctuary wall parted. At the pulpit, before some 1,700 worshipers in the church, stood Pastor Schuller. Over the speaker came his greeting: "This is the day the Lord has made. We will rejoice and be glad in it." The chancel choir ushered in a worship period that was over almost before Anne realized it.

That afternoon, after she had told her husband about the sermon, she shyly said to him, "The minister spoke about a pastor's class tonight. I would like to go, and . . . " "I'll go with you," he broke in. "I have a thousand questions to ask that preacher."

At 5:45 o'clock Frank and Anne joined 150 adults and children in a seventh-floor room in the Tower of Hope for the first session of a pastor's class. The Reverend Harold F. Leestma, co-pastor, introduced himself and presented his subject. Frank listened. On the way home he told Anne, "That man answered 500 questions for me today."

Three weeks passed. Anne and her new-found friends prayed

that Frank would come to know Jesus Christ. Midway through the fourth class period Mr. Leestma engaged the prospective church members in a discussion of faith. A young girl declared that she loved Jesus. A retired gentleman cited instances of answered prayer. Frank rose to his feet and everyone heard him exclaim: "I've found him!"

At the seventh and final class period, Frank, Anne and the other prospective members met with Mr. Leestma and three church elders. "Is Jesus Christ your personal Savior and Lord?" Leestma asked. With one voice they all replied, "Yes, truly, with all my heart!" Then Leestma gave them their first assignment: "Before a year passes, each one of you win one to Jesus Christ."

The church's organized evangelism program is directed by Leestma and the Reverend Eugene Pearson, who came to Christ as a teen-ager in the church, attended college and seminary and became a staff member in 1970. Leestma conceives the church's 6,000 members as a "movement." "We have 6,000 missionaries," he says. "We urge our people to put in a good word for Jesus once a day."

For Anne and Frank, getting involved at Garden Grove meant worshiping at one of three morning services, or at sunrise in an inspirational service led by Dr. Raymond E. Beckering in the "Chapel in the Sky." They became regular attenders at a couples' Sunday School class taught by one of the 350 Christian education volunteer workers.

Early in 1969 Frank went to be with the Lord whom he had so recently learned to love. Two years later Anne became one of 600 adult members of Garden Grove enrolled in the "Bethel" series, a two-year Bible survey course. At the midweek class Anne met a number of new friends, including Mrs. Jeff John, who was studying to equip herself as a "New Hope" telephone counselor. Mrs. John is one of 225 Garden Grove members who have received special training from a Los Angeles psychiatrist. When a person in need of help dials "New Hope," he contacts one of two counselors on duty in the Tower of Hope. Pastor Schuller appointed Dr. Beckering, minister of family and parish life, to direct this unusual program.

Bob Schuller himself was born in 1926 to a Dutch farm couple in Alton, Iowa. His father had cherished the hope that God would give him a son who would become a minister. This dream was not shared until Bob had graduated from Hope College and Western

One of the world's most unusual churches, Garden Grove Community Church attracts thousands of people each week who worship in pews or automobiles. Above, Pastor Harold Leestma, minister of evangelism, leads a membership class. Pictured at right is Pastor Robert Schuller.

Theological Seminary in Michigan. As the father put it then to his son, "I wanted *you* to make the decision."

Bob confessed Christ publicly at age 16 at his confirmation. Later his real goal in life came into focus while writing a paper for seminary. "I asked God for the chance to build a church from the bottom up," he says. In 1950 he was ordained a minister of the Reformed Church in America and was called to a church in Ivanhoe, Illinois. Dr. Beckering preached the ordination sermon. Five years later, pastoring in Los Angeles, Dr. Beckering nominated Schuller as pastor of a new mission church in Orange County.

The Schullers arrived in Orange County in February, 1955, with a small electric organ and $500. If the neighborhood canvass was disappointing, the search for a meeting place was even more so. However, a drive-in theater was available, and soon announcements began to appear: "On Sunday, March 27, at 11 a.m., church services will be held in the Orange Drive-In. Come as you are in the family car."

A choir from a sister church came to help. Fifty cars appeared "out of nowhere." Eighteen months later the Garden Grove Community Church moved into a new chapel three miles away, but the consistory (the church governing board) decided to maintain drive-in services at the old location. Each Sunday after church Schuller would tow the organ to the drive-in for services there. "A dream started evolving," he says. "Why not merge the chapel and the drive-in congregation in one big inspiring creation?" The present facilities are part of the fulfilment of that dream.

A 6,000-member church is able to provide very active programs for groups that are often not adequately cared for by the average church — a singles group, young couples, college age. In 1969 Dr. Beckering formed a class for divorcees, and 12 enrolled. Two years later 484 single, divorced and widowed men and women are registered in Sunday School groups just for them. College-age boys and girls, many in street clothes, began taking part in contemporary worship in the tower chapel during 1971. David Kirby, bearded elder of a Christian commune in Garden Grove, said, "At first, on outward appearance, this church looked real plastic to us. But we came here and found the people honest and real."

Twelve choirs under the direction of Sheldon Disrud are making Garden Grove Church a singing people. The elementary grade children devote one-half of their Sunday worship hour to the learning of hymns and church music. Two thousand children from nursery age through sixth grade are enrolled in a family-centered Sunday School curriculum under Miss Charlotte Heinen's supervision. An average of 306 junior and senior high school youth attended Sunday School at the church in the fall of 1970, some one hundred of them in a "Seminar '70" — a lively outreach meeting dealing with youth conflicts and the claims of Christ. It was directed by Ken Harrower, youth minister.

Dr. Henry Poppen and his wife, Reformed Church missionaries to China for 33 years, direct ministries with people of retirement age, called "Keen-agers."

In an "Institute for Successful Church Leadership" which Garden Grove hosts three times annually, Schuller emphasizes "the four principles of successful retailing: accessibility, surplus parking, inventory, and service with a smile." "The church is the only institution on the face of God's earth," says Schuller, "that can tell guilty people, 'Here's the way to peace: the way of the cross.'"

Schuller, who received an honorary doctorate from Azusa Pacific College in 1970, preaches messages aimed to meet the average person "where he hurts and show him how his problems can be resolved through a personal relationship with Jesus Christ." He asked the Reverend Kenneth Van Wyk to come and direct the Christian education program at Garden Grove Church in 1962 and charged him with the responsibility of helping every church member get hold of the truths of God's Word. Says Van Wyk, "We are ultimately preparing for an academy of lay studies at Garden Grove, similar to a basic seminary course, which will enable the layman to work his way toward becoming an adequately trained Christian."

Garden Grove seems to be well on its way toward becoming a church of the laity. The church's lay people offer 100,000 hours of volunteer labor in a year's time. "By 1975 we will have 10,000 members if present trends continue," Schuller says, "and we will need 600 trained lay pastors to care for them, one for every eight families."

Garden Grove followed up over six hundred referrals from the Billy Graham Crusade held at Anaheim Stadium in 1969. Many of these were among the 800 new members received during 1970. Sixty-five per cent of all new members come on profession of faith in Christ for the first time, or by reaffirmation.

A sizable percentage of Garden Grove's income (1970-1971 budget: $1,200,000) goes to missions, much of it for Christian work in the Orient. Dr. Schuller visited Asia in December of 1970 to challenge his people to put "The Hour of Power" on TV in Tokyo, in Japanese. The church has helped launch 13 new congregations in California. "The biggest contribution we make to solving social problems is to let Christ change people's attitudes," remarks Schuller. "But we do not stop there. Our people are teaching classes for the mentally retarded, helping illiterates through the Laubach techniques, and distributing tons of food each year.

"We are trying to set up here," says Schuller, "a team management on a large enterprising basis for Jesus Christ. If I'm still alive by the year 2000, I will be 74 years old. I hope I am. I expect to be addressing a group of young ministers and saying to them, 'While it is a thrilling thing to feel the power and the impact of the enormously strong church in America today, some of you would never believe that in the 1960s and the early 1970s leaders of the church in America were predicting its demise. They were predicting that the church of the future would be away from grounds and buildings into small homes and private cells and commune groups. How wrong they were. Only the established churches with building and staff and people and program can form a base for operation for the generations to come.'"

Mount Zion Missionary Baptist Church

8

8

Mount Zion Missionary Baptist Church

Los Angeles, California

Awake, awake; put on thy strength, O Zion.

For several years that verse has charted the course of Mount Zion Missionary Baptist Church of Los Angeles, California, in the heart of south central Los Angeles, which includes the Watts and Avalon communities.

Only a few years ago south central Los Angeles, home of 450,000 black citizens, was a blazing torch. Thirty-five deaths resulted from the week of rioting. Arson, looting and wanton destruction caused losses of over $200 million. Today Watts is quiet; wide streets and lovely parks create an atmosphere of apparent peace. Yet among civic leaders the possibility of another riot, more disastrous than in 1965, is never counted out.

At the corner of East 50th Street and Hooper Avenue, near the center of the riot area, stands a modestly appointed sanctuary presided over by a husky, dedicated, Bible-preaching young minister, Edward Victor Hill. The story of that church today is very much the story of the man.

When Edward Hill became pastor of Mount Zion in 1961, the church had liquidated much of its notable spiritual history and was snarled in quarrels and lawsuits. Members had lost heart. The church's very existence was at stake. Hill was invited by a former church member to come from Mount Corinth Missionary Baptist Church in Houston, where he was ministering, and preach at Mount Zion.

Three hundred people came one summer Sunday morning to

hear Hill preach. Most of them returned that night. "I reminded them that their sign read 'Mount Zion Missionary Baptist Church' and I just asked if their sign was telling the truth. 'Is this a *missionary* Baptist church?' Having learned of their differences I asked them, 'Suppose some young person comes here looking for a church and finds you carrying on like this?'"

Dr. Hill's first task was to train workers to replace those who had departed. "Even now our emphasis is on instruction, not enrolment." He has written the Bible lessons for high school and adult departments of the church school to impart to his people specific knowledge of Christian doctrine. Children study lessons published by the National Baptist Convention U.S.A., Inc., with which Mount Zion is affiliated. Church school attendance averages 350 pupils on Sunday morning.

Dr. Hill believes that "a strong church is a Bible-regulated church, a Christ-centered church, a prayer-powered church." Three of the church's six choirs lead the congregation in the two-and-a-half-hour Sunday morning service. Hill's sermons, packed with Scripture and meaning, are punctuated with "Amen's" from the deacons. An invitation to receive Christ is extended at each service. The congregation observes the Lord's Supper at the first Sunday evening service of each month, at which time new members are baptized.

One is made to feel that the same grace of God that was given to the churches of Macedonia (see 2 Corinthians 8) has been given to Mount Zion. In 1970 the congregation finished building its third dormitory at a National Baptist school in Africa (one in Liberia, two in Lesotho). It supports 40 children in a mission school in Jamaica. The church's budget grew from $30,000 to $140,000 in ten years, and membership stands at approximately a total of 1,200 persons.

Mount Zion has taught the basic message of Christ to more people through vacation Bible schools than by any other means. In 1968 its teachers reached 7,000 children in summer Bible schools. Twenty-three Southern Baptist college students (19 of them white) lived in the homes of Mount Zion members for two weeks and helped conduct these schools. Mount Zion's membership is organized in 28 geographical circles, each of which sponsored such a school last summer. "We had 164 of our people involved simultaneously," says Hill. "They enrolled 1,500 children from every nook and cranny. Children met in the church, in parks and in garages. One member had 84 kids in her back yard. Altogether 300 youngsters made decisions for Christ."

In December 1970 Dr. Hill witnessed the realization of one of his dreams. The first class to enrol in the World Christian Training Center, which Hill launched in 1969, completed six weeks of training. "They are the vanguard of an army of Christian witnesses through whom we intend to saturate the Negro community with the message of Jesus Christ," says Hill.

The World Christian Training Center acts as a "campaign headquarters for Jesus." Its goal in 1971 was to train 1,000 block workers for Christ. Hill unashamedly patterns the strategy of the Center after a political campaign.

"Our purpose," he says, "is to produce active and vital churches." In August of 1970, 1,207 young people, Campus Crusade for Christ workers, took a religious survey in a 100-block area in the black community and led 654 people to Christ. Within two days a letter from the Center, plus follow-up material, went to each home.

Biweekly evening classes are now held at the Training Center in the South Broadway Professional Building. Trainees study six subjects: "Who Is Jesus Christ?" "How to Receive Jesus Christ," "How to Lead Others to Christ," "How to Turn Your Church to Soul Winning," and "How to Reach Your Family for Christ." Teachers are drawn from a pool of 100 volunteer Bible teachers and Christian school faculty members residing in southern California.

By graduation night half of the first 40 graduates reported they had already been used to win some person to Christ. Miss Heddy Yearby told of witnessing to companions on an elevator that became immobile between floors. Clyde Morgan accompanied the Reverend Joseph A. Ryan, executive director of the Center, on a block survey one Saturday during the training program. Morgan witnessed to one of his neighbors in Compton. Two weeks later the man went to church and professed his faith in Christ.

"The Negro preacher," says Hill, "spends his time not only preaching the Gospel and winning souls, but in working with the unique problems of his membership." He found that the greatest problem facing his people was frustration — "knowing that what you need is available but not knowing where to get it." Some channels have now been made available to help them get what they need.

One such channel is The United Benevolence Society. Member-

Mount Zion Missionary Baptist Church is the hub of an entire community, and its pastor, Dr. E. V. Hill (standing at podium), is one of Los Angeles' leading citizens. At right, Dr. Hill inspects a new senior citizen complex being erected by the church.

SERVE THE LORD WITH GLADNESS
HAVE
FAITH
GOD HAS THE
POWER

ship is open to anyone, and some three thousand people in 72 California churches now enjoy the major benefits of membership: consultation, group insurance and group purchasing. The Society is "one of the few hopes for low-income people," Hill believes.

Christmas is an unusual time at Mount Zion. "We do not give presents to relatives," Hill explains. "We do this on their birthdays. We do not swap presents among ourselves. We discourage big dinners on Christmas Day. We do not approve of Christmas trees. Christmas cards are usually sent to unchurched individuals and backsliders." Church members are encouraged to give gifts to Jesus instead, by sharing with those "on his list" — the disadvantaged, the mission fields, those in prison and others.

The E. Victor Villa and Mount Zion Tower provide low-cost housing for south central area residents. Two more projects on the drawing board are a halfway house for parolees and a series of ten boys' homes. "Several hundred children, who have committed no offenses, are forced to live in detention wards in Los Angeles because there are not enough foster homes," says Hill.

If the pastor is particularly mindful of fatherless children, it is because he was reared by foster parents. His mother and father were divorced when he was a young child. From school age he lived in Sweet Home, Texas, in the two-room log cabin of Mr. and Mrs. Aaron Langrum, farmhands who had no children of their own at home. In Sweet Home, a black community near Seguin, in Guadalupe County, Hill was known as "sort of the boy of the town." He did chores for many of the families. He milked five cows every morning and earned an extra 50¢ a week for building the fire each day in the schoolhouse stove. Agriculture was his favorite subject in Sweet Home High School, which had 200 students. He was active in the 4-H Club and showed prize stock in the livestock shows in Texas. (At that time black youth could not compete in the calf division of the larger livestock shows — only the hog division!)

Of his segregated Sweet Home upbringing, Hill recalls, "We never had any bitterness. We were told the white man simply had the upper hand. But when World War II ended and our boys came home and told of another world, where Negro people are accepted as they are, I had my eyes opened." At age 17 Hill "preached his first revival" in Los Angeles and was elected president of the new National (Negro) Baptist Youth Conference. He enrolled in Prairie View A. & M. College, Texas, at that time a black institution. Resentment toward the white man was building up within him. "I became convinced that the real Christians were Negro people."

As a leader of Baptist students on the Prairie View campus, he was invited to accompany two black and three white students to a Baptist student convention in Nashville, Tennessee, in 1953. "I was filled with misgivings as to how the trip through the South would turn out, because we would all be traveling in one car." Dr. W. F. Howard, director of the Southern Baptist student ministries in Texas, was the driver. He said that they would stay together and eat together. "If there are places that will not serve all, we will not eat at all," he said.

"For the first time in my life I became acquainted with a white man who was Christian enough to take a stand with a Negro man who was a Christian," said Hill. "I discovered that there was another world, and that within this Christian world were some blacks and some whites who had been regenerated, so that the color of a man's skin really made no difference to them. I saw myself in the same condition I had seen much of the white community to be in, filled with 'churchianity' and justification of the flesh, but void of the Spirit of God. On this trip and at this meeting I invited Christ to take complete control of my life."

Hill met his wife, the former Miss Jane Coruthers, at Prairie View, where she received her bachelor's degree in nursing education. Hill earned his B.S. degree and later was honored with a doctor's degree by Houston's Union Baptist Theological Seminary.

Administrative assistant to Pastor Hill is Edward Bass, who has worked closely with him since 1963. At this writing, Mount Zion's ministerial staff is incomplete. "We are looking for a director of activities," says Hill. He does not rule out the possibility of adding a white person to the staff (three whites have served with Hill at Mount Zion), especially since only three hundred blacks are presently studying in seminaries in the United States, far too few to meet the normal needs that exist in the 40,000 Negro Baptist churches of America.

Hill, a former president of the Los Angeles Housing Commission, was elected unanimously by the city council in 1970 to the city's fire commission, of which he is now president. He was the organizer of the Congress on Evangelism held in Kansas City, Missouri, September 1970, and master of ceremonies at Honor

America Day in Washington, D.C., July 4, 1970.

In a decade when "polarization" is taking place among many races, and when "integration" has become an undesirable goal to radicals of black and white ethnic groups, Mount Zion is standing firmly on the promises of God and the love of Jesus Christ for all men. We can only say to this church of Jesus Christ in a restive part of America — and to every church — "Awake, put on thy strength, O Zion."

Concordia Lutheran Church

9

Concordia Lutheran Church

San Antonio, Texas

Where the fertile plains of South Central Texas give way to the rolling bush country lies the city of San Antonio, "cradle of Texas liberty." The 15th largest city in the United States, San Antonio is an unusual blend of old Mexico and young America. Forty-five per cent of its 654,000 inhabitants are of Spanish descent. Its four Air Force bases and the Brooke Army Medical Center stamp it as youthful, transient, defense-minded. The Alamo, hallowed to Texans, a monument to one of history's notable stands, has turned the city into a major tourist center.

From the year 1718 when San Antonio de Valero became the capital of the Spanish province of Texas, San Antonio's people have shown a deep religious sensitivity. In this hospitable setting in the last 20 years a church has grown and shared its enthusiasm for the Lord Jesus Christ and his Kingdom as have few churches of our time. It is the Concordia Lutheran Church, pastored by the Reverend Guido Merkens.

Born in Aberdeen, South Dakota, the son of a scholarly Lutheran pastor, Guido Merkens grew up in a strong church atmosphere. He was 24 years old when he went to San Antonio in 1951. Pastor Merkens still remembers, upon his graduating from Concordia Lutheran Seminary in St. Louis, Missouri, what his roommate thought of Guido's call to Texas. "He was going to New Guinea and was convinced he had the 'better' call," says Merkens. "And if I had known that I would live 20 years in a city with no major league team, I might have been inclined to agree with him!"

The pastor had been a three-sport letterman in college.

"But," he added in a serious vein, "my primary work has been here, and one thing God has taught me is, 'My word . . . shall not return unto me void.'"

In 1950 a religious census of north San Antonio revealed that the area was high-potential soil for the planting of a church. Merkens and his wife, Barbara, arrived in June, 1951. Within three months he had visited over two thousand homes. On December 16, 1951, a congregation of 37 charter members formally banded together to form Concordia Lutheran Church. In a chapel built on farmland by the members of this young church, the new congregation began its service to the San Antonio community.

On December 1971 Concordia marked its 20th birthday. Its baptized membership has increased to 3,000 persons, 2,100 of whom are communicant members. The church is known as the fastest-growing congregation among the 6,000 parishes in the Missouri Synod since 1951.

Where horses once galloped with their colts on the old Kessler farm, Lutheran school children now scamper, and hundreds of young people and adults take to Concordia's gymnasium and lighted ball fields for recreation and athletic competition. Where a barn and a windmill once stood, a modern worship and education complex now graces the ten-acre Basse Road site. When the sanctuary was completed in 1955 the Church Architectural Guild of America named Concordia an award winner among America's middle-sized churches. The sanctuary, constructed of a sand-toned Mexican brick, has since been enlarged four times to the present seating capacity of nearly one thousand.

As word spread throughout the Texas district of the growth of this San Antonio congregation, Pastor Merkens was asked to share what he calls "Living Lutheran Leadership" with other parishes. In 1965 he and Arthur Samuel, superintendent of the Concordia Sunday School, began traveling to other states, holding seminars eventually with 125,000 pastors and laymen in 44 states. "The seminars grew out of years of practical experience," says the pastor. In a 350-page manual Merkens spells out procedures for "evangelism," "edification," "stewardship," "admiration," and other ministries. In 1971 Pastor Merkens accepted invitations from Lutheran churches in England, Australia and New Zealand to conduct seminars with clergymen and lay people.

What commodity does this pastor and church offer to San

Antonio? "We have a sound, evangelical belief that appeals to people at this time — a solid faith anchored in the Word of God and trusting for salvation through Jesus Christ," answers Bill Wagner, managing editor of the *San Antonio Express and Evening News* and a church council member. Someone else says "*esprit de corps.*" The pastor would say, "It's the lay people." The laymen say, "It's the pastor." Concordia is what Izaak Walton might call the "compleat church" — serving, witnessing, caring, singing, exalting God, giving careful attendance to his Word, and doing all of this with contagious joy and gladness in the Holy Spirit.

Entering the sanctuary for the 8:45 morning worship service one Sunday, I sensed what one member described as "a feeling of power in the gathered congregation." Here and there worshipers knelt at their pews in silent prayer. The Concordia Day School Choir, a group of 55 fifth and sixth graders, sang the processional that lifted the mood to praise and signaled the beginning of corporate worship. Robed in cassock and surplice, the Reverend Theodore Graalmann, visitation pastor, led the order of worship. The congregation joined in responsive readings of the Old Testament lesson and the Gospel. After the united confession of the Apostles' Creed came "The Matter of Importance."

"This is something we learned from the Baptists," the pastor explains. "It is a way of bringing a matter of importance to the attention of our people for their support in prayer and for their edification." On the day of my visit Pastor Merkens asked Mr. and Mrs. Elmer Juelg and their five children to come forward, after which he conducted an impressive commissioning ceremony, setting them apart for missionary support with the Lutheran Bible Translators in Liberia, West Africa.

The most important part of church life to 75 per cent of Concordia's members, according to a congregational poll, is the sermon. The congregation stood for the reading of the text: "I beseech you therefore, brethren, by the mercies of God, that ye present your bodies a living sacrifice, holy, acceptable unto God, which is your reasonable service" (Romans 12:1). The sermon was inspirational, Biblical, well illustrated, simple enough for the young person to understand.

At the 11 o'clock service the anthem, sung with authority by the 60-voice adult choir, carried the theme of the morning sermon:

Missouri Synod Lutheranism is at its finest at Concordia, San Antonio. Far right, a portion of the Concordia Day School. Far right, volleyball is an important part of the broad church youth program. Pastor Merkens is pictured at right.

God of grace and love and blessing,
Thine alone shall be the praise.
Give us hearts to trust Thee truly,
*Hands to serve Thee all our days.**

Mrs. Rhoda N. Canion is the organist and director of the adult and the four Sunday School choirs. She is a graduate of Concordia Teachers' College, River Forest, Illinois, and a sister of the pastor. "When we were young," she recalls, "Guido played the clarinet and I the piano and we would work up concerts for Mom and Dad."

"From Dad I gained a tremendous respect for the Word of God," says Pastor Merkens. "When a man stands up to preach he had better put his whole heart into it. He must be excited in his own way, and he had better tell his people loud and clear what Jesus Christ means." Pastor Merkens was made a vice president of the Lutheran Church-Missouri Synod in 1971 and has preached on "The Lutheran Hour" international broadcast, but he is first and foremost a shepherd of souls.

Church members and visitors register their attendance in worship each Sunday. Before the following Sunday a member of the parish calls on the visitor in his home. One day while paying such a call, Ramona Stevens, head of the Women's Doorbell Ringers, noticed that the lady showed unusual interest. "I watched Billy Graham on TV from Oakland last night," she told Mrs. Stevens, "and I want to make my commitment to Christ." The 15-week adult instruction class was starting the next Sunday morning, and she became a part of that group of 60 adults. Assistant Pastor Stephen A. McClintic teaches the class. A majority of those attending become active members of the church.

A variety of services attract people to Concordia: the day care center, the elementary school, the vacation Bible school (last summer's school enrolled 911 children), and an aggressive sports program. Softball, volleyball and basketball teams from Concordia are regular winners in the city church league, and as the saying goes around the church: "They come to play; they stay to pray."

A geologist, Bob Keahey, and his wife and five children visited Concordia in 1963, searching for a church "that was not ashamed to proclaim Jesus Christ boldly." At Concordia they found what they needed. Later when Keahey began teaching in the Sunday

**From 'God the Father, Son and Spirit,' in the Chapel Choir series, ed. by Carl Schalk, ©1961 by Concordia Publishing House, St. Louis, Missouri*

School he was "scared to death" to pray aloud. "Pastor told me to talk to God just the way I talk to a good friend," he says. Keahey now calls each of his 35 ninth graders every week and is one of 11 teachers in the Young People's Bible Class. Attendance in this division increased 15 per cent in 1972; almost three hundred teen-agers are enrolled.

Sunday School and worship weekly attendance averages 2,750 children, young people and adults. On Wednesday night Sunday School teachers study methods and consider the Bible lesson for the following Sunday. Dr. Harold Meador, a dentist, shares the fruit of his Bible research with first- through eighth-grade teachers.

Concordia Lutheran School began as a kindergarten in 1952 and has developed into an accredited elementary school, with ten teachers and 317 pupils. Because Texas public schools do not yet offer kindergarten, Concordia provides a special service for parents who want early training for their children, says Principal James H. Boriack. Each year a number of families become members of the church as a result of this initial contact with the school. Over half the pupils in these modern classrooms come from Concordia families.

Something of what the school means to church members is indicated by newspaperman Wagner: "The school gave our son, Steve, a firm foundation on which to make the decision to enter the ministry." He is one of three young men from Concordia serving as vicars in a one-year internship before completing his final year at seminary. Twenty of the church's sons and daughters have entered or are preparing for the Christian ministry. Lenten offerings provide scholarships for every young person entering Christian training.

"Saving faith is personal, but never private," says Guido Merkens. He believes that those who criticize organization must admit that the Spirit can breathe through structure, and that "what is everybody's responsibility is no one's responsibility." He also believes that Satan is "pulling out all the stops today, but that when the world is at its worst, God will see to it that the church is at her best."

Paul describes the church "at her best" as a body "fitted together perfectly . . . each part in its own special way helps the other parts, so that the whole body is healthy and growing and full of love." Concordia is one congregation striving in the Spirit toward that goal.

First Assembly Of God

10

10

First Assembly Of God

Memphis, Tennessee

As the city bus stopped and started its way through the busy streets of Memphis, Tennessee, a young passenger attempted to open conversation with the gentleman alongside and found that he was completely deaf. The young man began using sign language and his seatmate smiled and "signed" back a warm greeting. After they had conversed a while in their silent language, the young man inquired, "Do you know Jesus Christ?"

"No," came the answer. "I'm from California and I don't know anyone in this area." Taking his cue, the young Christian proceeded to tell his new friend about Jesus Christ, using his hands as he had been taught in an instruction group at Memphis' First Assembly of God. The good news that he shared had been acquired under the tutelage of First Assembly's senior pastor, the Reverend James Ewell Hamill.

Memphis might be called the buckle of the Bible belt. Capital of the Mid-South, the city is not exactly a center of Pentecostalism; yet many of her spiritual leaders would agree with a Baptist minister's remark that when Dr. Robert G. Lee retired in 1959 after 33 years as pastor of Bellevue Baptist Church, the mantle of church leadership fell upon James Hamill.

The First Assembly of God began as an independent church in 1907 under the leadership of Pastor L. J. Adams. In 1914, when the Assemblies of God was formally organized in Hot Springs, Arkansas, Adams was present with one of his laymen, Ralph Riggs, who later served many years as the general superintendent of the Assemblies. The Memphis church affiliated with the newly formed denomination after a few years and experienced normal growth in the succeeding decades.

However, when the church issued a call to Hamill in 1944 it had been without a pastor for 15 months. The congregation had dwindled to less than a hundred members. Hamill, who had pastored churches in four states and was in the midst of an evangelistic ministry, was contacted by the church. "When I returned their call," Hamill said, "the board was actually meeting at the church. The chairman remarked to me, 'The Lord must be in this.' There were no stars in my eyes when I said I would come. The future didn't look great, but I felt in my heart, 'This is it!' " He was installed as pastor of First Assembly in December, 1944.

The 31-year-old pastor spent nearly every evening during his first seven years in Memphis calling on the homes of local residents. In 1948 the church sold its property on South Third Street, and moved into new facilities on East McLemore. As a result of a 1950 Oral Roberts campaign, the church received the names of many people who had asked for spiritual help. "We followed up every one, and many gave evidence of being committed to Christ," says Hamill.

In 1958, while looking for property for another church (one of six Memphis churches First Assembly has helped to found), Pastor Hamill was shown a seven-acre tract of land on North Highland in east Memphis. Four years later, on this attractive site in the center of Memphis' growing population, a new modern facility was dedicated to the glory of God. Like churches all over America, First Assembly was caught up in the shift from the city to the suburb. This was a sociological tragedy involving racial and other factors. In its new location some Negro children attend Sunday School and a few black families occasionally worship there. "Our welcome extends to everyone," says Pastor Hamill.

If one were to review the church's history he would conclude that 1971 was First Assembly's best year only because it was the latest year. Membership in 1971 registered a net increase of 150 persons and Sunday School attendance averaged 1,158 pupils, with high growth in the single adults and young couples' classes. Several new ministries were inaugurated during the year. A professional counseling service was reactivated under the guidance of the associate pastor, the Reverend Wallace Weber. An extension campus of Central Bible College, Springfield, Missouri, was opened with 39 students attending classes in the church's new 30,000 square-foot activities and education building. Memphis State University accepts up to 12 credits from courses taught in Bible, theology and Christian education. A Teen Challenge center was established in Memphis through the leadership of First Assembly. Its ministry is devoted to the rehabilitation of youth. In January, 1972, the church subscribed its largest budget, $501,000. Plans to establish an elementary school are under consideration, says the Reverend Kenneth Mayton, minister of education.

How did it all come about? The answer is found in seven factors that Hamill believes are essential to building a church. "The most important is spirituality," he says. "A spiritual church declares a simple message to people, telling them that they can have their sins forgiven and their burdens lifted. When people attend our Sunday School, for example, they study the Bible. Our music program is built upon the philosophy that music is not a display of talent but a ministry."

The second factor is personnel, the people who make up the church leadership and the staff. The other five factors are organization, facilities, follow-up, promotion and "plain, hard work."

I was listening for one factor that I did not hear. "What about missions?" The pastor answered quickly, "The seven factors build the church. Missions is a result." The Memphis congregation has a worldwide ministry. The church gives $125,000 annually toward the support of 65 missionaries and some fifteen overseas projects, including Bible schools in Belgium, Italy and the Philippines, and orphanages in Egypt and Korea. Approximately sixty young people from First Assembly have entered full time Christian work, and are strongly supported daily by the prayers of the church. The junior and senior high school youth staged a roller skating marathon in the spring of 1971 and raised $400 for Rev. and Mrs. Jerry Sandidge. Sandidge, a former minister of education in the church, moved to Europe in 1972 to minister among college people.

Memphians are church-going people and on Sunday evenings many of them go to First Assembly. There they hear the Word of God and share in a popular and well-executed program of Gospel music. Ken Carter, the director of music, was formerly a soloist with Canadian evangelist Barry Moore and the Air Force "Singing Sergeants." A son of the church, he now oversees the

Built on traditional Pentecostal lines, the First Assembly of God, Memphis, brings a spiritual ministry to a great city. At right, Reverend Hamill (right) and his staff. Lower right, after school activity in the church's modern gymnasium.

activities of the church's eight choirs, in which some three hundred singers are involved.

Sundays at First Assembly climax in the prayer room, just off the 1,700-seat sanctuary. "This is where the battle is won or lost," says Pastor Hamill. "Many people who attend our Sunday evening evangelistic rallies are not Christians. They come a few times and soon they are conscious of something here that they have not discovered elsewhere. More than once, as they have tried to pray following the meeting, they have realized that they do not know the Lord. Someone in the Prayer Band 120 (patterned after the disciples in the upper room at Pentecost) prays with them. These people often become active in other churches, but some of them tell us, 'Here it was that I found the Lord, and here I want to remain.'"

Pastor Davis superintends the prayer room where as many as 200 people may be kneeling at one time. The mood is reverent. The only sounds are those of audible prayer here and there and occasional weeping. "We certainly believe in expressing our feelings, but we don't emphasize the emotions," David says. "Rather, the presence of the Lord is what is essential."

Pastor Hamill is one of 13 men who comprise the executive presbytery of the Assemblies of God. He was born April 15, 1913, in Winston County, Mississippi, one of two sons of a timber contractor. His father died when James was six.

"Mother took us to the Methodist church every Sunday," he recalls, "but not until I was almost 16 did a service made any impression on me. Mother had remarried and we were living in Meridian. One Sunday afternoon I was with some young people who invited me to attend church with them that evening. The choir in that Pentecostal church appeared to be the happiest people I had ever seen. Maybe that's why I love music to this day. I don't remember what the preacher said, I was so eager for him to finish his sermon so I could go forward. At the altar I knelt and shed tears for the way I had been living. A few people prayed beside me.

"Two weeks later a flu epidemic closed down everything in Meridian and I lay in bed with a high temperature. The pastor came to our home and prayed, and God healed me. A few days later a neighbor lady said to me, 'I believe the Lord wants to fill you with his Holy Spirit,' and I told her, 'If you think so, why don't we get on with it?' That night I knew God wanted me to preach the Gospel."

Hamill was ordained at 19 by the Assemblies of God. His first pastorate was in Columbia, Tennessee, where he met a pretty Virginia brunette, Katheryne Stone, who later became his wife. They now have two married sons.

Thanks to modern communications media, Pastor Hamill has become almost as well known to Memphis as its famous son Elvis Presley. He has been on radio and TV longer than any other minister in the city. In 1947, three years after becoming pastor of the First Assembly of God, Hamill went on the air with a daily broadcast over WHBQ radio and in 1955 the church began a weekly television hour on WHBQ-Channel 13. "Christ Is the Answer," now simulcast each Sunday in color on TV and on AM radio, is a bright half-hour of music and spoken word in Pastor Hamill's direct style.

"We used an interview format when we first went on TV," says Hamill. "My guest on the first program was a converted whiskey salesman who was then delivering milk. One couple who viewed that program were on the verge of separation. They called on me at the church, and told me that if Christ could change the life of a liquor man, maybe he could save their marriage. They took their first step toward God that day and they are still happily married."

In 1970 the pastor had a narrow brush with death. Lab reports showed that he had malignant tissue on one lung. The people believe their pastor was healed in response to fasting and prayer. God evidently had several more things he wanted to accomplish through James Hamill. One of his goals is to increase First Assembly's annual gift to world ministries to $500,000 by the close of this decade. And why not? As he tells his people every week, "All things are possible to him that believeth."

First Alliance Church

11

11

First Alliance Church

Mansfield, Ohio

"I had been asking God's forgiveness for my sins and I went to other people and asked them to forgive me, yet I harbored deep resentment and unforgiveness within myself. Now I know that this has caused a depression that for years has been as real as cancer to me. But praise God! I feel the battle is over and the victory is won!"

The words were spoken by a married woman whose life had been changed in the revival that was moving through the First Alliance Church of Mansfield, Ohio, in the early days of 1972. Pastor William E. Allen had invited the twin evangelists, Ralph and Louis Sutera, who had recently moved to Mansfield, to preach on Sunday evening, January 2. Under their ministry numbers of Christians in Saskatoon, Saskatchewan, had been spiritually reawakened.

Louis Sutera told almost one thousand people gathered at First Alliance to call sin *sin* and to break with anything the Spirit convicted them of. As parents, teen-agers and children responded, a spirit of revival broke out. Animosities and hard feelings between persons of the same family and among church members began to dissolve. The service continued with prayers and testimonies until 1 a.m.

The following Sunday morning as 750 worshipers observed communion, opportunity was afforded the people to testify, as is the custom, while the elders served the people in the pews. For two hours ushers passed a wireless microphone among those who wished to speak. "I have been praying in unbelief," stated one woman. A physician said, "I have been stiff-necked about my personal business. Little things have built up so that I couldn't tell my family I loved them." "The TV was taking over my life," confessed a housewife. "I had no patience with the children. How could I tell them of Christ if they could not see him in me?" A young boy testified, "I have been stealing sweets at Dad's store."

The pastor never got to his sermon during the service that evening. Many of the 600 persons present went to the altar; a time of sharing continued until almost midnight. A 17-year-old girl told the congregation that Christ had delivered her from witchcraft. "For the first time in my life, I am experiencing freedom such as I have never known," she said. A young woman in the choir expressed what must have been felt in many hearts: "There's a great big smile inside that won't go away."

If the Spirit of God was sweeping through First Alliance Church in the early months of 1972 it may have been because of what had happened over the previous five years. Pastor Allen calls it "a deep moving of God" among his people.

This congregation of fewer than five hundred has given birth to two other churches since 1960. In June, 1970, almost one hundred members had voluntarily left First Alliance to form a new congregation in Bucyrus, 20 miles west of Mansfield. The same thing happened nine years earlier. Today 51 young people from First Alliance are enrolled in colleges and Bible schools. Thirty laymen, trained under the disciplined leadership of their pastor, are visiting in the homes of the community each week.

The church began as the Grace Tabernacle under the leadership of Dr. L. H. Ziemer in 1916, meeting first in a park and then in the YMCA. During Dr. Ziemer's six-year pastorate the congregation laid the foundation of a church on East Third near the city square. The sanctuary was completed in 1940. Three years later the church affiliated with the Christian and Missionary Alliance, a denomination that was founded as a missionary society by Dr. A. B. Simpson. In 1956 William E. Allen became the church's seventh pastor.

The parsonage on Brinkerhof gives the impression of lively congeniality, and no wonder! The Allens have ten children. Allen himself has an "old shoe" attitude of friendliness that makes him well-liked in the community. Born in Succasunna,

New Jersey, he grew up in Dayton, Ohio, the oldest of four children. His family was without a knowledge of the Gospel although his parents took the children to church and Sunday School.

As an agnostic student at De Pauw University, Greencastle, Indiana, during the pre-war years, Allen attended a Nazarene church simply "to make a psychological study of the people." Their sincerity impressed him, but he continued to maintain an aloof attitude and poked fun at "religion" in his class assignments. In 1941 he graduated and married Madonna Wills of Dayton. Subsequently he became a Sunday School superintendent in the devout belief it would help him sell more insurance.

His mother-in-law invited him and his wife to the Burns Avenue Alliance Church to hear the Reverend Paul McDowell in February, 1942, and he consented to attend on one condition: "Promise never to ask us again." The Allens attended two meetings, and on the third day Allen spent four hours with McDowell. "I had my nose in the Bible all the time," recalls Allen. "Every question I asked Mr. McDowell, he answered from Scripture. I knew that if the Bible was true, I was a lost soul."

At home that evening, under strong conviction, Allen made up his mind to go to church that night and give his heart to Christ. "I was sure it would cost me every friend I had," says Allen, "but I was willing." That night, as the choir sang "Softly and Tenderly, Jesus Is Calling," he went forward and made his decision public. He later learned that his mother-in-law had been fasting each week and had been praying over a two-year period for his conversion.

Allen soon sensed a call to preach, and spent three years at seminary, including two years at Asbury Theological Seminary in Kentucky. Subsequently he was called to pastorates in Eaton, Ohio; Racine, Wisconsin; and Rochester, New York, before going to Mansfield in 1956.

Five years later the church had outgrown its building, but expansion was out of the question at the time. At an Alliance district meeting Allen heard missionaries describe the dividing and multiplying of their churches in Thailand. (The Christian and Missionary Alliance, though a small denomination, has approximately nine hundred missionaries at work in 41 countries.) Allen returned to Mansfield and suggested to his people that they start a new church. Within the year the church purchased

First Alliance Church, Mansfield, Ohio, has sent out hundreds of revival teams throughout America. The staff, above, is not large but the prayer volume, upper right, is remarkable. The Reverend William E. Allen, seated above, is pastor.

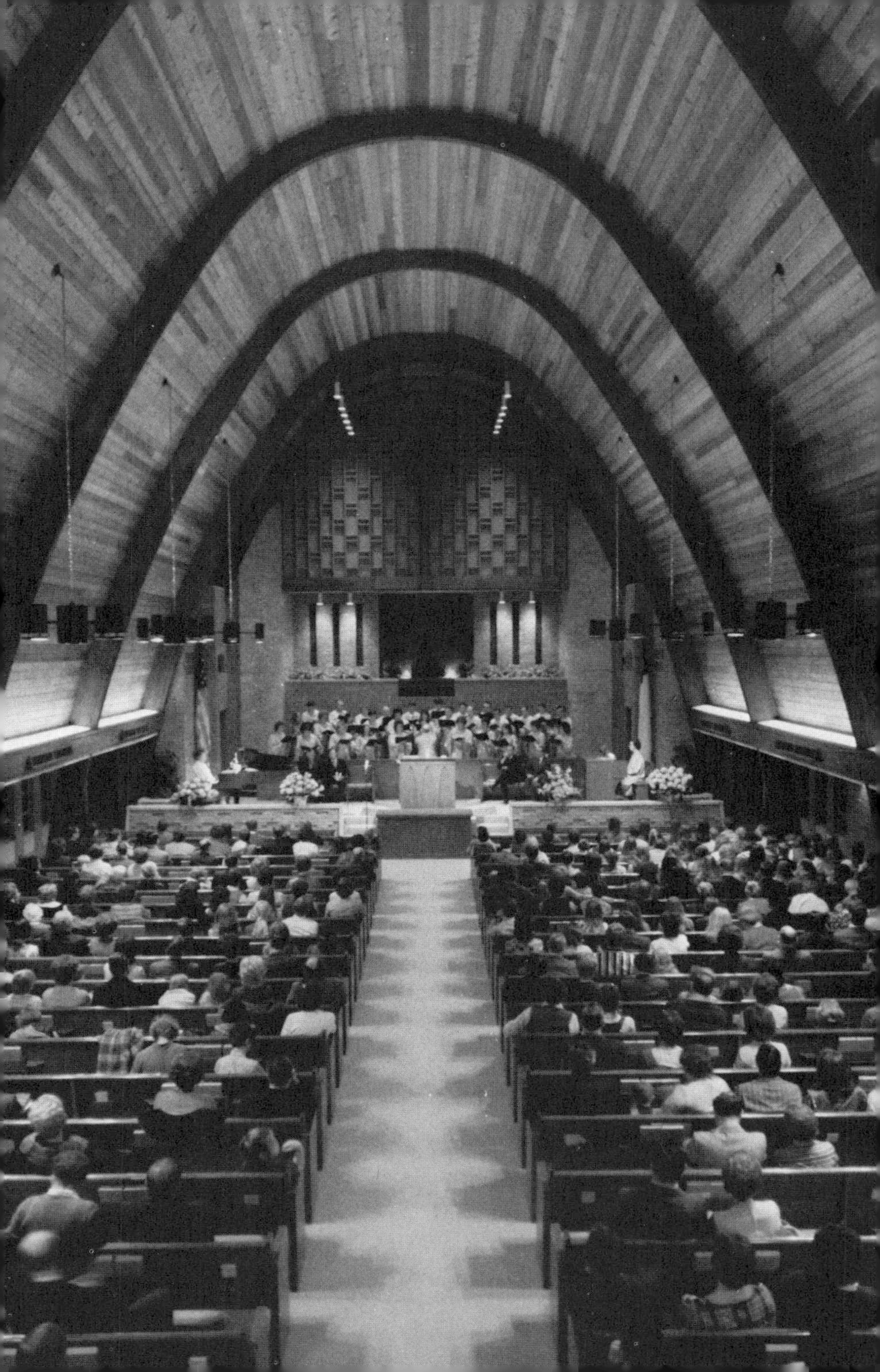

five-and-a-half acres of land, erected a building, and sent 96 of its members to form the Westwood Alliance Church. "In the 'hiving off,' 12 members of our 22-voice choir went with the new congregation," says Allen. "But the following Sunday instead of ten people in our choir there were 32. Divine mathematics!"

In the congregation's 50th anniversary year, 1966, the church moved to its present location on three acres in an area of 1,000 homes. The beautiful edifice on West Cook Road made growth an attractive possibility; prayer and a plan made growth a reality.

In 1965, after reading Robert Coleman's *The Master Plan of Evangelism,* Pastor Allen had prayed for three weeks for specific guidance in carrying out the mission of the church in Mansfield. Then he selected certain men of the church and asked them to rise a half hour early five days a week to seek God's will in prayer and in the Scriptures. He also asked them to remain for an hour after prayer meeting on Wednesday nights to learn how to lead a home Bible study and how to witness, and to pray with him for one hour before Sunday evening services. Twenty-one of the men accepted his challenge for a six-month period. At one time 12 home Bible studies were meeting weekly. A Bible study group meeting in a farmhouse in Bucyrus became the nucleus of the new church that was formed there in 1970.

In a four-month period in 1966, 26 new families united with the church. A podiatrist who became a new member at that time came up with a suggestion for a "junior deacon" ministry. This now involves 30 men who systematically visit the members of the church and also make evangelistic calls on visitors. "We have 30 assistant pastors instead of only one," says Allen.

The pastor's weekly column in the Mansfield *News Journal,* "It's the Truth," attracts many visitors to First Alliance as does the closely graded Sunday School program staffed by 28 teachers and workers. Attendance in Sunday School averaged 390 people in 1971, almost capacity in the present facilities. Two books are in constant use at First Alliance, the Bible and the *Hymns of the Christian Life.* The people follow Allen's expository messages closely. Five tuneful choirs led by George McNair lend a touch of heaven to every service.

Pastor Allen gives opportunity in the evening services for informal testimony, asking if anyone would like to share what Christ has done for him that week. Bob Hawkins, an insurance man then unconverted, was attending such a service when the pastor spoke those words. "I was shocked," Hawkins says. "I wasn't aware that Jesus had done anything in the last hundred years. Five people stood and I was amazed by the way they spoke of Christ. During the sermon, as the pastor referred to different Scriptures, the people leafed through their Bibles to find the verses." In a matter of weeks salvation had come to the Hawkins' household.

"In 1961 God led me to begin a Friday morning businessmen's prayer breakfast," Allen says. Some sixty men have found Christ through its ministry. When Ohio State's All-American quarterback Rex Kern spoke at the prayer breakfast a few years ago, 545 high schoolers and businessmen attended.

A world map inlaid in the terrazzo floor of the church foyer bears eloquent witness to the world outlook of this Mansfield congregation. In its history the church has given $800,000 to overseas missions and has sent many sons and daughters into the Lord's service. One young man who grew up in the church, Charles Holmes, was called as assistant pastor two years ago. In 1970 one of the church's young women went to Ban Me Thuot, Vietnam, as a missionary nurse. One year a supervisor at the local Fisher Body plant resigned his post, and he and his wife entered Campus Crusade's lay ministry.

As the witness of this modest-sized church in Ohio's rolling hill country goes onward, God has added a spirit of real revival. The revival has spread and other churches have been set aflame by Jesus' love. Who knows? As Pastor Allen expresses it, "Mansfield may become known as God's Field."

First Baptist Church

Van Nuys

12

12

First Baptist Church

Van Nuys, California

It was the kind of warm evening in Van Nuys, California, that brings middle-aged shoppers, young lovers and thrill-seeking youths to the boulevard. City police, answering a complaint at a "nude bar," found a pack of teen-age boys and girls kneeling on the sidewalk. "What's going on?" they asked. One boy who seemed to be a spokesman for the group replied, "We're praying that God will close down this dump."

The police left them alone and it encouraged the youths. They upped the volume of their prayers and began sharing Christ with the customers, almost all of whom by now had forsaken the activities inside for the spectacle outside. In time the incensed proprietor was at the door, demanding an explanation: "What are you trying to do? Close me down?"

As two of the young men went inside to explain, one of them was heard to say, "Man, we want to keep you out of hell. We're here to tell you about Jesus Christ." The audacious teen-agers proceeded to witness on the sidewalk, leading five of the bar's patrons to Christ. Before leaving, the group announced a New Year's Eve march on Van Nuys Boulevard. A few weeks later, New Year's Eve, 1970, the proprietors of two bars in that block closed their doors for the whole night.

"They probably sensed that the police would give them no protection from these Christian kids," smiled Harold L. Fickett, Jr., pastor of the First Baptist Church of Van Nuys, which sponsors the "Mustard Seed" coffeehouse two doors from one of the bars.

Such frontal attacks on Satan's strongholds are a way of life at First Baptist. The Biblical images drawn from the tiny mustard seed — enormous growth and mountain-moving faith — seem uncommonly appropriate to any description of the church.

Three years after the Van Nuys townsite was officially opened in 1911 in northwest Los Angeles County, a mere "seed" of 15 people gathered in a railroad chapel car (named *Emmanuel*) and formed a congregation. Today their "faith in God is becoming known around the world" (Romans 1:8, LB).

The soil in which First Baptist took root was the San Fernando Valley, which was to become a forward-looking community and a center of the aerospace and motion picture industries. When Evangelist Porter L. Barrington was called to be pastor in 1947, First Baptist had grown to 1,500 members and had helped a half dozen other churches get started in the Valley. In the next 11 years Dr. Barrington baptized 2,323 new believers. Before poor health forced him to resign in 1959, duplicate services were instituted to accommodate the people coming to worship at the present location on Sherman Way.

In the months just prior to Pastor Fickett's arrival in Van Nuys in July, 1959, the congregation experienced its only serious internal discord as it sought to determine its Baptist affiliation. "'Preach' [as the pastor is affectionately called by close associates] got us all working so hard and so fast," says Dr. John Gustafson, minister of music since 1955, "that within a month we forgot we had any differences." The church adopted a policy to become independent, cooperating with various Baptist conventions.

Under Dr. Fickett's energetic leadership First Baptist Church has grown to 10,000 members. Its Sunday School is one of the ten largest in America with 3,600 children, young people and adults studying the Word of God each Sunday. In 1965 the congregation dedicated a 2,000-seat sanctuary in which duplicate services are held Sunday mornings.

In 1972 the church occupied the five-floor Bennett Building, a Christian education unit. A 12-story senior citizens' residence will be constructed in 1973. First Baptist operated in 1972 with a budget just under $2 million. The heart of the church is a highly motivated, spiritual staff of 70 full-time and 87 part-time employees. Regal Books has just published the pastor's *New Hope for Your Church,* which sets forth ten principles of church growth.

It is the story of the Van Nuys church.

The only child of a Baptist minister, Harold Lord Fickett was born in Tucson, Arizona, and grew to young manhood in Galveston, Texas. At Baylor University, where he matriculated at the age of 16, he showed winning form in tennis, capturing first place in the Texas junior tournament. He considered becoming a professional tennis player or a lawyer. In his sophomore year, being uncertain, he sought counsel from Dr. J. B. Tidwell, his Bible professor. The old gentleman asked Fickett, "Did you ever get down on your knees before the Lord and tell him if he wanted you in the ministry, you would be happy to go?" Fickett agreed to do it. "Back in the boarding house I told the Lord just that," he says, "and almost as if someone had spoken to me, I felt this was what the Lord wanted me to do." Bible became his major and while at Baylor he pastored his first congregation, a little "half-time church" in San Gabriel.

In 1938 Fickett graduated with high honors from Baylor and entered Southern Baptist Seminary, Louisville, Kentucky. After completing 33 months of active duty as a Navy chaplain, he studied at Eastern Baptist Seminary, where he earned a doctorate in theology. He and Mary Frances Dorsey of Nacogdoches, Texas, were married in 1940. Following pastorates in New Jersey, Pennsylvania and California, Fickett served historic Tremont Temple in Boston, from which he was called to Van Nuys.

"When I came to San Fernando Valley in 1959," he recalls, "the public schools were running out of space, so we opened an elementary day school. Now 400 children are enrolled for the school year." Described by the pastor as a "unique evangelistic opportunity," the school has as its principal Dave MacKerron, who had served as youth minister under Fickett at Tremont Temple.

If the day school was started to meet a need, the same could be said about the church's ministry to the Jewish community, the Spanish- and Hungarian-speaking communities, groups of handicapped persons and the day care center.

In 1967 a young car club enthusiast, Thom Piper, accompanied some First Baptist young people to the church's retreat grounds in the San Bernardino Mountains. "I went along to wreck the camp," he says, "but I was converted to Christ." Today Piper heads up FAM, "For All Mankind," a church ministry bridging the gap between the drug culture and Christ. FAM, the coffee-

First Baptist Church, Van Nuys, places a tremendous emphasis on youth and music. Dr. Harold Fickett, pastor, is pictured at right center.

NO
PARKING
ANY
TIME

house, and a family counseling center are incorporated under an "umbrella" organization, The Shepherd's House, operated by the church.

This church makes maximum use of mountain and beach resorts to reach young people for Christ. Instead of condemning Little League ball on Sundays, the church has organized its own Saturday sport programs. The three ball fields and Barrington Gym are in constant use as boys and girls from all over the Valley participate. "At the end of a sport season we invite the youngsters and their parents to a hamburger feed," says MacKerron, who is minister of weekday activities. "There we show them 8mm movies of their games and share a testimony to the power of Jesus Christ."

MacKerron also coordinates activities for the "Jolly Sixties," retirement age adults who devote almost 100,000 hours of volunteer work to the church annually. Some of the Jolly Sixties conducted an evening service in a nearby church and 13 teen-agers responded to the invitation.

Shortly before Christmas, 1971, an 80-year-old lady found Christ through the witness of one of the church's volunteer workers who call in convalescent homes. Within three weeks she had read the entire large-print New Testament given her by the church. She told the worker, "I'm going to visit my unsaved sister for a few days, and I want to know what the Scriptures say so I can talk with her."

Commitments to Christ are recorded almost daily through the church's pastoral care ministry, Sunday School visitation, high school and college youth outreach, and Sunday services. A total of 481 new Christians came into the membership of the church in 1971, presenting the staff with a monumental task of follow-up. The challenge is met by channeling all young persons and adults into a continuous seven-week class in doctrine taught Sunday mornings by Loy Coward. A lay man or woman goes to the home of each new convert and assists him in a basic eight-week Bible study.

Wednesday evenings Dr. Fickett leads some six hundred adults in 30 minutes of intercession followed by 50 minutes of instruction from one of the books of the Bible. Meanwhile the Sunday School staff is meeting in departmental groups. "We go in with the idea of planning every minute of the Sunday School hour so that we can make an impact on the lives of our people," explains Charles Smith, minister of education. "The teachers are helped to become learning stimulators rather than lecturers." Smith is teamed with a corps of age-group directors who administer a "culturally relevant and Bible-centered" program of Christian education.

If visitors to the First Baptist Church were asked, "What brought you here?" chances are most of them would say "the music" or "the preaching." An extraordinary music ministry has developed under the creative hand of Dr. Gustafson, tenor soloist who admits to "some flair for production." Thirty-five choirs involve more than 1,500 singers in the church. The "Amen Choir," 140 adult voices accompanied by the Casavant pipe organ and grand piano, makes the 11 o'clock worship hour a high point of the church's life. The college and high school choirs sing on alternate Sundays at the earlier service.

Fickett moves around behind a pulpit rail pleading God's case before his hearers. (He once aspired to be a lawyer.) His sermons are expository and simply communicated. Not afraid to spend hours in his study, Fickett commits each sermon to memory. He preaches for decision.

"We are a program church," says Gustafson. "Everything is done to move the heart toward the acceptance of the preaching once we have drawn people into the house of God." The "Living Christmas Tree," a spectacular musical program featuring the college choir singing from a 50-foot-high "tree," was presented nine times during a recent Christmas season to meet the demand. Pastor Fickett extended an invitation to receive Christ at these musicals.

Since 1967 Gustafson and "The Certain Sounds," 26 college-age vocalists and instrumentalists, have been communicating with young people on the West Coast through the medium of song. In July, 1972, they shared their enthusiasm for Jesus Christ over television in Osaka, Japan; in Seoul, Korea; and in Hawaii, where the 1971 team spent five weeks. "Usually the 'Sounds' are accompanied by a support team of young people who are trained in witnessing and follow-up," says Gustafson. "When we have presented a package of music, these kids witness to individuals in the audience. Three couples who participated in 'The Certain Sounds' ministry in 1971 returned to Van Nuys and made plans to enter full-time Christian work."

In addition to "The Certain Sounds," the congregation supports some two hundred outreach ministries in southern California and worldwide. Four young people from the church were engaged in camp and evangelistic work during the 1971 summer months in Hong Kong and Italy and, as a special project, First Baptist is helping to erect a hospital in Kalimantan, Borneo. "Each year the missionary part of our budget is increased a greater percentage than is any other portion," says Fickett.

The pastor stresses four reasons for the blessing of God on the Van Nuys church. "The organization of our church, not so much a democratic body as a republic, enables the boards and staff members to act when they believe God is leading," he says. "First Baptist has been known for several decades as 'a church with a vision.' It's no mere slogan; these people operate on faith. God provides the staff as it is needed. We believe he intended the church to be a service institution. One of the prayers of my life is 'God, deliver me from being a professional preacher. Help me to realize I'm only a servant of Jesus Christ.' Until Jesus comes back, which could be any day, we will go on serving him by serving our fellowman."

Holy Trinity Church

13

13

Holy Trinity Church

Adelaide, South Australia

Evangelism is the cornerstone of the ministry of Holy Trinity (Anglican) Church of North Terrace, Adelaide, the pioneer church of the state of South Australia. Here the first church service was held under a ship's sail on the first day of the year in 1837. During the 100-plus years that have since elapsed, thousands of persons have come to a personal knowledge of Jesus Christ at Holy Trinity.

Close links have always existed between this historic church and the state, and the governor still formally approves the appointment of each new rector. One front pew is known as the governor's pew, and it is often occupied by a party from Government House.

Trinity is a historic building, but it is through its people that the church's message is made relevant. More than one thousand persons attend the Sunday services, and the church membership numbers almost two thousand. The building buzzes with activity every day and night of the week.

At the center of it all is the rector, the Reverend Lance Rupert Shilton, whose preaching has been the heartbeat of the church for the past 14 years. In addition to his pulpit ministry and consequent nationwide commitments arising from it, Shilton is an author, a newspaper columnist, and a radio and television personality.

After his conversion to Christ as a young man at a youth missionary meeting, Shilton studied for the ministry at Ridley College, Melbourne, and completed his arts degree at the University of Melbourne. He was called to be minister of St. Jude's Carlton, Victoria, where he served the congregation of an industrial suburb before going overseas for further study at the University of London. In 1958, as chairman of the local Evangelical Alliance, he joined in inviting the Graham Team to Adelaide for a Crusade the following year. Joan Shilton, his wife, a former nursing sister, is continuing her university studies. They have two young daughters.

Three curates assist the rector in his responsibilities: The Reverend Tony Tress is in charge of pastoral work, the Reverend Graham Knight works with young people, and the Reverend Hugh Prentice coordinates the educational program. Four wardens and a parish council of 12 men guide the church program through the work of various committees. Many committees are chaired by laymen with expertise in a particular field. Hundreds of lay men and women contribute their skills and talents to the life of the church.

At present 25 young men and women of Holy Trinity Church, some with their families, are serving Christ abroad, either as missionaries or lay personnel. They are in South America, East Africa, India, Pakistan, Vietnam, Hong Kong, New Guinea and Arnhem Land. Missionary giving at Holy Trinity is among the highest in Australia from a single congregation. Almost one-third of the church income goes for work outside Holy Trinity itself. Hospital patients, prisoners and pastors in underdeveloped countries are studying the Bible through correspondence courses based on the weekly lessons taught at the church.

The old church has kept pace with contemporary needs and has sometimes led the community. One significant instance was their opposition to the performance of the controversial musical *Oh! Calcutta!* a protest that led to the show's cancellation in Adelaide. Mr. Shilton and the people of Holy Trinity, with other concerned people, provided strong leadership in that incident.

Today the geographic boundaries of the parish run through commercial and industrial parts of the city square mile. The congregation, however, gathers from suburbs all around Adelaide in response to the direct and simple presentation of the Gospel with its call for personal conversion. While the message proclaimed at Holy Trinity has not changed, the methods of presenting it are constantly being revised and improved as new needs are recognized.

A widening of outreach has had an impact on the local community and has established a notable ministry overseas. Through Holy Trinity's Overseas Bible Correspondence Fellowship an Englishwoman came to know Jesus Christ after having moved to Adelaide. Her son's friend, an African theological student in London, received the Bible studies and then passed them on to her son. He wrote to Mr. Shilton asking that he contact his mother after her arrival in Adelaide. She began to attend Trinity. The clear message and the warm friendship she found there showed her the meaning of her son's faith. She too became a Christian and entered the life of the church.

In 1959 Mr. Shilton introduced "guest services" to which church members bring their friends and special groups from the community. More than eight hundred inquirers have committed their lives to Christ through these services, and many of them are now key people in the life of this church and other churches.

Adelaide holds a Festival of Arts every two years. At the Festival Trinity produces a program with a Christian theme which has been of such high quality that it is recognized as an official Festival attraction. In March of 1972 a stage presentation, "Dream of Kings," contrasting the discovery of Tutankhamen's treasures and the empty tomb of Christ, was presented by a cast of 60 church people. Hundreds more helped in staffing the exhibition, conducting tours of the church, ushering, booking seats, and serving tea to visitors. One talented church member spent hundreds of hours making magnificent headdresses and costumes. Coordinating all this was the public relations committee (chaired by Warden Philip Coward) which arranged the publicity and worked with other groups to tie it all together.

Outside the church on Sunday mornings stands a mobile trolley where coffee is served and where the people greet newcomers. The visitors who wish to join Trinity are invited to a "welcome evening" held every two months at the home of a warden or parish councilor.

Such an evening was held at the home of Ray Kidney, the church organist and the secretary of the Prisoners' Aid Society. During the evening of music, talk and a short film of events at Trinity, young people mixed easily with older folk. Mr. Shilton explained the program of the church, and Mr. Kidney read from Colossians and led the group in prayer. Further opportunity for fellowship followed at supper in the garden.

At the "welcome evening" some members told why they had

Holy Trinity's ministry extends into many directions including social actions (note protesters below) and a Festival of Arts, right. At middle right is Sir Mark Oliphant, governor of South Australia. The Very Reverend Lance Shilton has since become Dean of Saint Andrew's Cathedral, Sydney.

IN THE LOVE OF GOD, AND HUMBLE CONFIDENCE IN
CHRIST HER SAVIOUR
ON THE 15TH DAY OF JUNE 1849,
IN THE 45TH YEAR
OF HER AGE
The memory of the just

first come to Trinity. One young man said he had been helped by reading "Guidelines," the rector's newspaper column. One young woman, who now has a ministry in music at Trinity, explained that she was invited to play the violin at a guest service. "I was not a Christian then," she said, "but I found the message so challenging and so plain that I kept coming and I found Christ." A bearded young man told what had happened to him. "I was a bit skeptical about church but my brother was a curate at Trinity, and I came here from Victoria. I thought I'd have a look at the place. I remember leaning up against the walls and thinking how strong they were. My life needed security. I talked with Hugh Prentice and he helped me. Then at a guest service I was converted. It certainly made a difference to me."

The education program of the church is designed to deepen the spiritual life of church members and train them for responsibility. A wide range of study courses is arranged for three terms during the year on Sunday evenings. The education committee also arranges a panel discussion each year on a controversial issue. Many people attend, and discussions follow on topics such as abortion, drug abuse and the permissive society.

Clergy and lay people alike share the duties of pastoral care. Trained visitors go to hospitals and homes where parishioners are sick. For most of the elderly and infirm, the monthly service of holy communion is their only outing and opportunity for worship. Volunteer drivers collect them for the service, and a special bus brings a contingent from the Home for Incurables who sit in the aisles in their wheelchairs. This has become known as Trinity's "spiritual meals on wheels"; more than 150 people find it a highlight in their lives.

Prayer is the lifeline of a church, and at Trinity it is woven into every aspect of church life. Even the group of women who meet each week to fold the church papers and service leaflets carry on a quiet ministry of prayer for persons in special need. Before guest services parishioners meet at prayer breakfasts on their way to work.

Every year 100 couples attend pre-marriage counseling courses. They receive guidance in financial, sexual and psychological matters, as well as in the spiritual life. Young married people from the church act as hosts and hostesses at supper and a number of the newlyweds later join the Trinity Marrieds Group.

Not all of the counseling is for those who will be married. Many people with deep problems seek anonymity in a city church, especially one whose minister has the reputation of being a wise counselor. Some people with social or psychological problems are referred to lay people with special abilities.

At Trinity the very young are catered for in a well-run creche so that parents can take part in study courses and services. The youth program takes in all ages up to young adults with fellowship meetings, sports, adventure camps and house parties during the year. After-church coffee and sing-alongs are popular.

Women, young and old, play an important part in the life of the church organizations, committees, home meetings, counseling and catering. The Women's Service Fellowship sends many gifts to the church's missionaries. The Mothers' Union gives opportunity for women to share and help each other rear their families as Christians.

Music is provided by a loyal and dedicated choir, with visiting soloists, and a junior choir which sings on Sunday mornings. Orchestral music, trumpet solos and guitar folk songs all help express the congregation's worship of God on special occasions.

Holy Trinity believes in communication. The two church papers — *Trinity Times,* for friends of the church all over the world, and *Trinity News,* for the resident congregation — keep members and interested people informed. Often individuals visit the church because of something they have read in Mr. Shilton's biweekly "Guidelines" column in the *Advertiser.* The rector's nightly meditations over station 5DN have been reproduced in book form; he is the author of several books on Christian living. More than one hundred thousand copies of sermons and addresses given by preachers at Holy Trinity have been distributed.

Holy Trinity ministers in the midst of change. Students who complete their studies and move on and lay people who relocate because of new work commitments serve as a reminder to this old church that the "times they are a-changin'."

The people's warden, Peter Smith, a surveyor with a growing family, put it well in his report at the vestry meeting. "As another year ends," he said, "we are reminded of the well-known words, 'Great things he has taught us, great things he has done.' Despite our small efforts in his service, God has chosen to use our church as a vital witness in this city."

Mount Olivet Lutheran Church

14

14

Mount Olivet Lutheran Church

Minneapolis, Minnesota

"Mount Olivet has become a central part of my life" — a widow.
"I talked it over with my wife after the Bible class, and we decided to take Jesus Christ into our lives" — an athlete.
"I've got to give the credit for this to God, but I think he has used you" — a counselee.

This is Mount Olivet, largest active Lutheran congregation in the world, located in the heart of Luther country — Minneapolis, Minnesota. Just why, in the providence of God, one among Minneapolis' 588 churches should explode in the mid-twentieth century into a membership of nearly eleven thousand communicants, many people have sought to explain.

They have pointed to sociological factors: congenial Scandinavian environment, favorable site on the city's growing south side, and so on. They have described the proliferating activities in which the church is engaged, and the administrative network that makes it all mesh — to the glory of God. Particularly they have emphasized the role of the late Dr. Reuben Youngdahl, under whose 30-year pastoral leadership the membership grew from 300 to nearly ten thousand members.

When a team from DECISION went to investigate Mount Olivet, however, it found more than all of these factors. It found more even that the warm evangelical Lutheran teaching so reminiscent, even after four centuries, of the great hero of the Reformation.

What it found was a church that cares.

Beyond the traditional Gothic lines of the beautiful sanctuary, erected in 1948, are to be found the marks of Mount Olivet's ministry: the Careview Nursing Home for 150 patients; Mount Olivet Home for 100 aged people; Rolling Acres, a $1 million facility for 60 mentally retarded children; Cathedral of the Pines, a camping facility not far from Lutsen on Lake Superior where as many as 1,800 young campers learn about Christ each summer; and Caribou Lodge, a cottage-type facility for Christian families, located adjacent to Cathedral of the Pines.

These corporate installations speak eloquently of a church's ministry that pushes past normal ecclesiastical boundaries to touch the life of a community at some of its most sensitive points. And that, according to Pastor Paul H. A. Noren, who succeeded Pastor Youngdahl in 1968, is exactly what Mount Olivet has in mind.

"Our community concerns," says Pastor Noren, "are so much involved with evangelism that they could in no way be considered duplication of civil or secular programs. For example, we are affiliated with the Midwest Challenge ministry to drug victims, sponsored by the Minneapolis Police Department through Al Palmquist. We are helping to sponsor Jack Stolfus in a 'discovery' program in some of our area high schools, which seeks to assist disaffected young people through a 'Young Life' type of approach."

Another local ministry which Mount Olivet supports (with a sister church, Augustana Lutheran) has enabled hundreds of inner city children of Minneapolis and St. Paul to enjoy weekend retreats at Highway House near Mora, Minnesota. Here children learn to prepare meals, help with farm chores, and participate in recreational activities such as swimming and horseback riding. The purpose of Highway House is "nonverbally to manifest the love of Christ in our relationships, and verbally to introduce the children to Jesus Christ."

Mount Olivet contributes to the support of individual missionaries and to the international mission program of its denomination, but is becoming increasingly involved in its home community. The social ministry committee recently added to the staff on a part-time basis the Reverend Linton Scott, originally from Jamaica. Specifically directed to the inner city residents and to minority groups, his ministry is "in a positive Christian spirit."

Mr. Scott describes his activity:

"I work mostly among the poor, but even among some affluent people, dealing with whatever their needs are. Most of these people are referred to Mount Olivet, and then to me. There are problems of runaway children, drugs, family disturbances, drunkenness, lack of food or clothing or housing. We always manage to get in an invitation to attend church. Our basic mission, of course, is to lead people into the Kingdom of God. The whole church is geared to that end, and I am happy to be a part of the Mount Olivet team."

When Reuben Youngdahl died suddenly on a world tour in 1968, many people expected the church to stagger under the blow. But as Pastor Noren says, "When Reuben built this church he built a real one." Paul Noren and Youngdahl had grown up together and had been seminary roommates. Mount Olivet called Dr. Noren from his pastorate in Denver, and at the same time called Reuben's son, the Reverend Paul Youngdahl, from his pastorate in St. Paul, to be the new associate pastor. These men, plus three other ministers, Dr. John G. Metzker, the Reverend Harlan N. Robbins, and the Reverend Carl O. Nelson, with 25 staff members, make up the Mount Olivet "team."

The message of Reuben Youngdahl was the traditional Gospel, as thousands who remember him will testify. (One of his friends was Billy Graham. In July, 1960, the World Council of Churches held a "consultation on evangelism" at Bossey, Switzerland. Among those invited to participate were Reuben Youngdahl and Billy Graham. They met in the Geneva airport, roomed together at the consultation, and found themselves in hearty agreement with each other on the subject under discussion.)

"The sermons Reuben Youngdahl preached at Mount Olivet," says Pastor Noren, "were utterly simple both in their development and in their delivery. They had a warm evangelical thrust that reflected not only his concern for people, but his love for the Savior. The books of meditations that he published each year are a testimony to his faith in Christ."

Dr. Noren preaches a sound Biblical message. That's not surprising — he served on the committee of the 1965 Colorado Crusade in Denver, and is serving as chairman of the Billy Graham Upper Midwest Crusade scheduled for July, 1973 in Minneapolis-St. Paul. "A huge Crusade is not the typical mode of evangelism in which Lutherans engage," says Dr. Noren,

Mount Olivet is big — with 11,000 members it is the largest Lutheran church in the world — but Mount Olivet's effectiveness is not in its size but in its penetration into every part of the Twin Cities.

"and yet we feel it is one way to bring people to Christ, and especially in this year of Key 73 we want our church to be represented and involved.

"Lutherans are not threatened by such an undertaking. We feel that this is another way in which Christ is glorified. Martin Luther considered evangelism to be at the heart of the Gospel, and so does Mount Olivet. I have found nothing but positive reactions on the part of our people to the Crusade that is now approaching — not one negative response. We admire Dr. Graham greatly and our people plan to volunteer for various duties in connection with his meetings."

Mount Olivet comes out of a warm, pious strain of Scandinavian Christianity. It was organized on January 21, 1920, with 20 charter members and 23 children, under the then Augustana branch of Lutheranism. This branch was deeply influenced by the revival movements of Hans Nielsen Hauge in Norway [see DECISION, April, 1971], and Carl Olof Rosenius in Sweden. Today it is part of the Lutheran Church in America (LCA).

As Pastor Noren explains it, the great contribution of Reuben Youngdahl was to foster a growing church, yet never to allow a distance or disinterest to develop between the pastor and the people. "The impersonality associated with a large church just isn't here," he says. That feeling is echoed by Paul Youngdahl.

"As I was growing up in the parsonage, I noticed how much my father enjoyed his work. This had a great impact on me mentally and spiritually. I had some mountaintop experiences during camping days at Cathedral Pines that led me to believe that it was God's will for me that I be a full-time servant of his; but I guess I always felt I wanted to be a pastor." At 36 years of age, with a brilliant basketball record behind him at Gustavus Adolphus College (he stands 6'7"), Paul Youngdahl is an important part of Mount Olivet's pastoral team. He oversees the worship and music areas, the camping program, and is part-time preacher.

The other pastors also share in the various ministerial duties, including house and hospital visitation. Reuben Youngdahl would make dozens of calls a day in the homes of his parish, and he set a pattern that has continued. But the great work of the church is not performed by the busy staff — rather it is done by the laity. Parish volunteers contribute about 81,000 hours a year to the program of the church. If that sounds as if it has the complexity of a modern corporation, it's not far off: Mount Olivet is six corporations. It is served by a church council of 49 members, has an annual budget of about $775,000, and a Sunday School enrolment of 2,000 pupils.

Perhaps no church in the world has quite the Sunday schedule of Mount Olivet. From 9 a.m. to 12:40 p.m. four complete services are conducted, each lasting 40 minutes. They are preceded and followed (at 8:30 and 12:45) by communion services. Cars are shuttled in and out of the parking lots with the help of 100 volunteers who direct traffic. On special days, such as Easter morning and Christmas Eve, as many as nine consecutive services will be held. The same minister (Dr. Noren) preaches each time, but the choirs alternate. Mount Olivet is famous among other things, for magnificent music.

Why the taxing Sunday activity? It all fits into the same schema: Mount Olivet is a people-centered church. It accommodates others instead of seeking to accommodate itself. It cares about the people who come and about the people who don't come: when the Key 73 home visitation was announced, the church sent 700 volunteers calling in the neighborhood.

"The mission of this church," says Dr. Noren, "is to be a lighthouse to direct men to Jesus Christ, and a guidepost to build them up in the faith." Through the doors of Mount Olivet some seven thousand people pass every Lord's day. They come from Minneapolis, St. Paul, and surrounding towns. Some have been Presidents: Lyndon B. Johnson was the last chief executive to worship there. Judges, doctors, scientists, airline pilots, are present each week. But there is also a little lady who lives in a poverty area on the north side of Minneapolis, who belongs to Mount Olivet — and comes regularly.

"I've got hundreds of friends here," said one man as he walked out of the sanctuary on Sunday morning. "It's like a great big family reunion every time I come to church." But Wendell Erickson, a prominent lay leader, put it differently. "The real drawing power of Mount Olivet is faith," he said. "People come here looking for faith. They want assurance that God will see them through their troubles, and that they will receive the promise of eternal life."

At Mount Olivet thousands find what they are looking for because the church cares enough to see that they get it.